4-8-70

Mealtime Manual
for the Aged
and Handicapped

Mealtime Manual

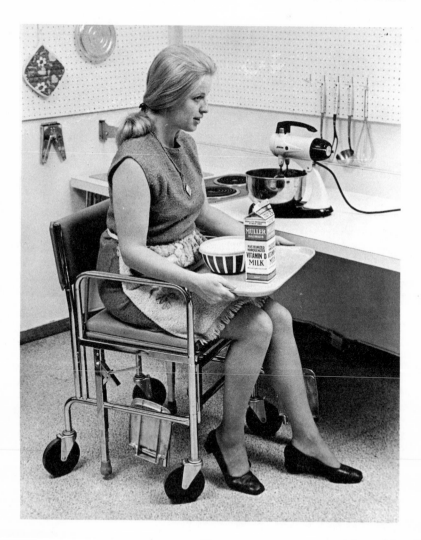

for the Aged and Handicapped

Compiled by the

INSTITUTE OF REHABILITATION MEDICINE
NEW YORK UNIVERSITY MEDICAL CENTER

JUDITH LANNEFELD KLINGER, O.T.R., M.A.
FRED H. FRIEDEN, M.D.
RICHARD A. SULLIVAN, M.D.

With a foreword by Howard A. Rusk, M.D.

An Essandess® Special Edition   New York

Dedicated to those stalwart homemakers who,
although limited by physical problems,
are unbounded in their ability and love in caring
for their families, and to all the patients
at the Institute of Rehabilitation Medicine
who tested procedures
and provided new answers and insights.

MEALTIME MANUAL FOR THE AGED AND HANDICAPPED

SBN: 671-10461-6

Copyright, ©, 1970 by the Institute of Rehabilitation Medicine.

Published by *Essandess Special Editions,*
a division of Simon & Schuster, Inc.,
630 Fifth Avenue, New York, N.Y. 10020,
and on the same day in Canada by
Simon & Schuster of Canada, Ltd.,
Richmond Hill, Ontario.

PRINTED IN THE U.S.A.

Foreword

There is a legend that an old man will starve to death if he doesn't have someone to cook for him, and an old woman will starve to death if she doesn't have someone to cook for. This is a truism that is generally accepted. If it is true for the aged, it is doubly true for the disabled. The reason is simple. "Crippled as I am, it's just too much trouble," is a typical response.

But just as men and women everywhere yearn to be free, so do they also strive to be independent. They want to be as self-sufficient and productive as possible, so that they can actively contribute to the society in which they live. Handicapped homemakers lead the rest of society in their struggle for independence.

During therapy sessions with elderly and disabled homemakers, we on a rehabilitation team teach techniques to help them perform tasks more easily and make maximum use of their energy and abilities. We teach them proper (and indeed essential) self-care and personal hygiene methods. And above all, we teach them the importance of good nutrition.

However, knowing all the facts about proper nutrition is not enough. People must be able to utilize this knowledge by planning well-balanced, daily menus—and then actually making the meals. Able-bodied people, with a short course in meal planning, can do it. The handicapped and the elderly have a few problems. Have you ever tried to peel a potato or separate an egg yolk from its white with only one hand? Without bending your knees, can you pick up food spilled on the floor? From a sitting position, say in a wheelchair, can you reach groceries on the top shelves in your kitchen?

Mealtime Manual for the Aged and Handicapped offers solutions for just such problems. This book, with its easy-to-follow meal plans and its kitchen-tested preparation techniques, should certainly help millions of handicapped homemakers who have no contact with rehabilitation personnel or institutions, and who struggle on their own to manage a home and family.

Mrs. Klinger and her co-authors have most effectively synthesized all the basic techniques and latest findings in homemaking experiences with disabled people. *Mealtime Manual for the Aged and Handicapped* culminates a unique two-year research project which was undertaken by the Institute of Rehabilitation Medicine, New York University Medical Center, through a grant from the Campbell Soup Fund. The research group was composed of medical advisors, two occupational therapists, a home economist, a bio-engineer, an electrical engineer, and a graduate engineering student. The answers they and their patients found are presented in this book as a fundamental contribution to handicapped homemakers. This is more than a scientific treatise. It is truly a labor of love and dedication.

—HOWARD A. RUSK, M.D.

Contents

Introduction

Every homemaker wants to streamline tedious jobs, but for those with physical handicaps, safe shortcuts are essential. This book is directed to those of you who have chronic conditions caused by disease or age, as well as to the newly handicapped homemaker who wonders "What now?" Realize that you are not alone; for example, there are over 12,000,000 women in the United States afflicted with arthritis. Providing good nutrition and tasty meals for you and your family requires more care and more planning ahead, but it actually can be done.

In May, 1968, the Institute of Rehabilitation Medicine, New York University Medical Center, received a grant from the Campbell Soup Fund to study the meal preparation problems of the handicapped and elderly. We decided to delve into two main areas: the packaging and use of convenience foods; and the design and use of small electrical appliances. We felt that these areas should be carefully studied for the possibilities they offered as well as the problems they might present. The time-saving features, consistent results, and the ease with which convenience foods may be stored in the freezer or on the shelf are helpful to any homemaker. Portable electrical appliances also offer assistance to the homemaker unable to change her kitchen to meet her physical needs.

Time, of course, limited the number of things we could test in each area. So we focused on container openings of the most popular types of packages, finding techniques that would allow you to handle them more easily. And we tested a variety of appliances, looking for design features and factors applicable to any appliance. We narrowed the scope to those that are most versatile and offer the most help in meal preparation. No affiliation with or endorsement of any company is intended by the selection of specific units.

The distilled information and tips in this book come from two major sources. New material was garnered from our research over the past two years. A second source, for information on basic techniques and equipment, has been the practical experience with handicapped women and men in our homemaking retraining program at the Institute. For almost twenty years now, individuals using only one hand, managing with two weak hands, or dealing with some other problem, have relearned tasks that allow them to be independent in caring for themselves and their families at home. Along the way they have given us ingenious ideas that we are proud to pass on to you.

A few of these homemakers come quickly to mind. Mrs. F., a young quadriplegic, confined to a wheelchair, helped with much of the testing before returning home to her husband and child. She showed how homemakers with loss of grasp in their hands could manipulate container openings and appliance controls. Mrs. W., a gourmet cook, who never says "no" to any meal idea, tested recipes to determine the problems that another homemaker with cerebral palsy or poor coordination might encounter. She and her husband, each with the use of only one arm, run a lively household. Mrs. H., a post-polio housewife, has minimal use of both hands and arms, and so uses her mouth to hold tools to prepare foods. As a working wife, she really depends on quick tricks. A specially designed cart permits her to move her equipment around the kitchen. Miss G., a rheumatoid arthritic, demonstrated the stresses that opening containers and handling plugs can put on hands impaired by weakness and joint damage.

We have not been able to change package or appliance designs. Rather we have given suggestions that will allow you to move easily and handle what is available. In two years, however, some encouraging changes have been noted. The representatives of several companies have watched films of women struggling to open containers or handling appliances with difficulty as knobs refuse to turn or shelves fall out. Private industry is beginning to explore better solutions with keen interest and perhaps, before too long, we'll see some of the results on the market for all of us to share.

Most of the equipment shown in this book is helpful for any homemaker, and therefore can be found in local stores. A list of sources is, however, given for the purchase of items harder to find or not available locally. See pages 229 to 236 for a complete list of all manufacturers mentioned in this book. Approximate and list prices are stated in all cases, with the understanding that they may change. Many items are available at discount. A suggestion card is included for you to send back. Any ideas or areas you feel we should consider for further exploration and study, or any tips you want to share are very welcome and will receive wholehearted attention.

If you face serious problems in handling your home, you may want to seek additional help. Depending on where you live, your doctor may be able to refer you to a therapist or nursing service through your local health department, a rehabilitation center, or a hospital out-patient service. Several agencies listed in the back of this book provide information in special areas. State divisions of vocational rehabilitation, under their program of job counseling, physical rehabilitation, and related services, accept some homemakers for assistance and training.

We would like to acknowledge and thank all those who have participated in the development of this book, including Mrs. Ellen Herbst, O.T.R., who worked on the research for the first year, William B. Murphy, Mrs. Carol Smith, George Sarkar, Myron Youdin, Karen Graver, Mrs. Joan Wilson, Stanley Simmons, Gene McDermott; our thanks also go to Babette Brimberg for rewriting and rearranging this book, and to all the patients who offered their time and suggestions.

The days of big, suction-based bowl holders and complicated, one-handed can openers are over. They have been replaced by the imaginative use of versatile items that are available commercially. Streamlining is in! Whether through the use of convenience foods or electrical appliances, the target is less time and energy expended, and more fun and creativity in your kitchen. As you find new ways to be quick-order cooks, we hope you'll let us know how you have harnessed technology's advances to your chariot. Happy cooking!

JUDITH LANNEFELD KLINGER, O.T.R., M.A.

Hints for the Elderly

The modern cook prides herself on finding shortcuts in her kitchen, no matter what her age. If you find that increasing age is slowing you up and making simple tasks seem more difficult and time-consuming, then it's time to readjust your ways of doing things. Throughout this book, you'll find tips that can be adapted to help you whiz through kitchen tasks more rapidly.

Proper nutrition is just as important for you now as it was when you were a growing youngster. Keep up your energy by eating a varied, balanced diet each day. Technological advances in food processing have put marvelous new products on pantry shelves. Rather than curbing your creativity, these convenience foods will help you create more excitement in your meals. Many of them come in single- or double-portion servings, which is especially handy if you are cooking for only one or two people.

Conserving energy is also important. Sitting while you work guards your legs and hips against fatigue, and prevents stress on the joints. The Admiral's chair from Yield House, shown on page 37, permits you to sit and work at a standard-height counter. Keep a stool under your feet for comfort. Use a wheeled table or cart to carry everything to the table in one trip. (See pages 120 and 121.)

Safety becomes increasingly important as you grow older. If your balance is not stable when you walk, or your vision is impaired, take extra precautions to avoid costly falls or accidents. A rubber mat next to the sink prevents skids. Keep a light sponge mop and long-handled dustpan and brush handy to quickly wipe up spills. (See page 64.) Be sure to wear suitable—and safe—clothing while you work in the kitchen. Sturdy, well-fitting shoes reduce fatigue, help posture, and provide surer balance. Long, loose sleeves are dangerous, as they can easily catch fire if you reach for a pan at the back of the stove. Don't light the oven while wearing a flammable nightgown or peignoir. Let the wisdom of your age manifest itself in the way you apply common sense and safety considerations to homemaking tasks.

1

FIG. 1 A lowered work counter and sink open underneath allow this homemaker with osteoarthritis to conserve energy as she works in her kitchen. She is able to slide items from the sink to the stove. The single-handle faucet on the sink responds to light pressure by either hand. Standard-height chairs on wheels are carried by office-supply and hospital-equipment companies, including Lumex and Hamilton Cosco.

Hints for the Homemaker Who Works with One Hand

If you've suddenly been faced with the problem of working with one hand in the kitchen, you may think that it's very hard. It isn't. Thousands of women, using just one hand, manage to care for their families and do all their household work by applying a few special techniques. Some of these women were born with only one arm; others lost an arm through amputation or as a result of polio or nerve damage. Most, however, had a cerebral vascular accident which caused hemiplegia or partial paralysis of the body.

To those of you with hemiplegia who are now using a wheelchair or walking with a cane, relearning mealtime tasks may seem difficult. Yet, when you think about it, it's surprising how often that second hand only stabilizes the food or pan. Actually the second hand usually keeps the things being cut, opened, or stirred from sliding around. For example, it prevents the skillet from skittering across the range, or the potato from dancing across the counter.

Included here are some simple implements that act as stabilizers.

Hemiplegia, as you probably know, is not just limited to an arm or a leg. Perception or awareness can be affected. Sometimes remembering how you used to do things, or even what you want to do, seems hazy. To combat this, it's best to write things down. Make definite plans or steps for each activity until you are used to doing them again. If you have lost your sight on one side (hemianopsia), you'll have to learn to turn your head to compensate.

The doctor may prescribe a sling to hold your arm in a more comfortable position at first. As soon as you can discard the sling, start using your arm to assist in holding. Place your utensils so that they are convenient for a one-handed approach. Take enough time for all activities. Sit down at work so you won't tire easily. Plan simple, one-dish meals that can be prepared ahead of time; rest up before adding final touches.

Sometimes aphasia, or difficulty in speaking and understanding, accompanies hemiplegia. This doesn't mean that you can't cook. Just take your time. At first, prepare simple dishes that do not require you to consult a cookbook. Then gradually work up to more complicated menus and recipes.

STABILIZING

FIG. 1 A board with two stainless steel nails for holding meat, vegetables, fruits, and other foods while you cut or peel them is a helpful aid. The board has a raised corner that will stabilize bread while it is being spread or buttered. Suction cups under

FIG. 1

the base prevent the board from sliding around. Sources, as well as plans for making your own, are given on page 202, under Sandwiches. For safety's sake, it's best to keep a large cork on the two nails when the board is not being used. Also see the rocker knife for one-handed cutting, described under Eating Aids, on page 125.

FIG. 2 A versatile sponge cloth not only does a good job of cleaning up, but when placed under a bowl while mixing, or a pan while scrubbing, keeps these items from turning. These cloths are absorbent, clean easily, and may be boiled to sterilize. They are manufactured by American Sponge and Chamois Company, Inc., and E. I. DuPont de Nemours and Company, Inc., and cost about 30¢ at grocery and variety stores. A whisk works as well as a one-handed eggbeater for mixing jobs. For batters, an electric mixer is less tiring. Here's another stabilizing hint: keep a filled teakettle on the back of the stove, to provide an instant anchor when you turn or stir food. Simply push the pan toward the teakettle; the handle will swivel to one side and stay there. (See page 169.)

BREAKING AN EGG

FIG. 3 To crack an egg with one hand, hit the side of the egg sharply against the edge of a bowl. Then use the thumb and index finger to push the top half of the shell up, while the ring and little finger hold the lower half down.

Separating whites from yolks can be accomplished with a funnel or egg separator, as illustrated on page 215.

OPENING CONTAINERS

FIG. 4 Your knees will come in handy as an anchor for boxes or bags of food to be opened. With still-frozen plastic bags, cut off the top with scissors, unless the item is to be cooked in its bag. If you're working with an immersible bag, place it on a plate, cut the top open with scissors or a serrated knife, and lift up the bottom edge of the bag to empty the contents.

FIG. 2

FIG. 3

FIG. 4

FIG. 5

FIG. 5 To release a jar top with one hand, set the bottom of the jar inside a drawer and lean against it with your hip. The base of the jar will remain steady while the top turns.

FIG. 6 When a jar is new or the cover is very tight, it is often difficult to stabilize it securely enough between your knees or in a drawer to open it. This Zim Jar Opener can be attached to the

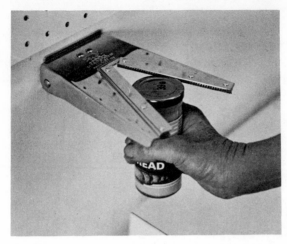

FIG. 6

wall in a convenient location near your work area. The deep wedge is lined with steel teeth that grasp the cover as you turn the jar. The wedge folds flat against the wall when not in use. A bottle-top pry opener is located along the top of the wedge to aid one-handed opening of bottles. Cost is about $3.75 at houseware stores, mail-order firms (including Rehab Aids), or directly from the Zim Manufacturing Company. Hanging the opener about one foot above a counter or small shelf gives a place to set the jar right after it is opened and prevents it from accidentally falling to the floor.

NOTE: Several similar wedge-type openers are commercially available, but many of these have only a narrow ridge of teeth and are of a softer metal so the teeth wear down quickly and do not grasp the can. The Zim Jar Opener will withstand years of use.

UTENSILS

FIG. 7 When using one hand to turn or lift foods, small kitchen tongs work better than a fork, as forks tend to stick in the food. Several styles of tongs are available from houseware stores or mail-order firms. Manufacturers include Ekco, Foley, and Feemster. Ekco's natural-angle tongs (Catalog No. 56KP), bent to keep hands away from heat and splatter, cost about 40¢.

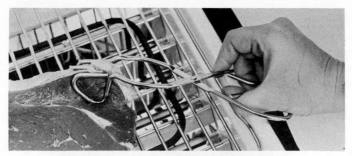

FIG. 7

FIG. 8

FIG. 8 It's difficult to lift and carry pans with one hand. Whenever possible, slide them to and from the sink and range. Once the pot is at the range, you can add water with a long hose from the sink or a large plastic cup. Ladle or spoon foods out rather than lifting a pot to drain. Several suggestions are given under Techniques and Recipes.

PUBLICATIONS PROVIDING FURTHER INFORMATION

EPISODE: REPORT ON THE ACCIDENT INSIDE MY SKULL. Eric Hodgins. Atheneum, New York, 1964. $5.

HELP YOURSELF—A HANDBOOK FOR HEMIPLEGICS AND THEIR FAMILIES. P. F. Jay, E. Walker, and A. Ellison. British Council for Rehabilitation

of the Disabled, Butterworths, London, England, 1966. $1.75 from
Appleton-Century-Crofts, 440 Park Avenue South, New York, New York.
10016.

STRIKE BACK AT STROKE. U.S. Department of Health, Education, and
Welfare, Division of Chronic Diseases, Superintendent of Documents,
U.S. Government Printing Office, Washington, D.C. 20402. 40¢.

STROKES—A GUIDE FOR THE FAMILY. American Heart Association, New
York, 1964. Distributed through local chapters.

UNDERSTANDING APHASIA: A GUIDE FOR FAMILY AND FRIENDS. Patient
Publication #2. Publication Unit, Institute of Rehabilitation Medicine,
New York University Medical Center, 400 East 34th Street, New York,
New York 10016. 50¢.

UP AND AROUND. Public Health Service Publication No. 1120. U.S. Department of Health, Education, and Welfare, Superintendent of Documents, U.S. Government Printing Office, Washington, D.C. 20402. 50¢.

Hints for the Homemaker with Weakness in the Upper Extremities

Weakness in the upper extremities may result from several causes.
If you have a chronic illness, you may find it tiring to lift objects, but
may be able to handle fine-hand tasks without any difficulty. A
person with muscular dystrophy or multiple sclerosis may have varying degrees of weakness, perhaps in the shoulders and hands, and
may tire very quickly. A person with quadriplegia experiences
loss of power in both the hands and arms, the amount of weakness depending on the level of the spinal cord lesion. Loss of grasp and release in the hands may be coupled with decreased elbow and
wrist strength. Trunk balance may be unstable due to paresis below
the level of the lesion.

Because of the wide range of disabilities that may occur, not all
the suggestions given here apply to everyone. Planning a counter at
a height comfortable for work and selecting lightweight kitchen tools
may prove an adequate solution for you. Or you may discover that
some tools or basic equipment will have to be adapted to your own
use. If you are in a wheelchair or suffer from a loss of sensation or
coordination, you will want to read the sections pertaining to you.

Also, the suggestions on kitchen planning, storage, and electricity offer concrete advice.

OPENING CONTAINERS

The wall-hung Zim Jar Opener, described in the section on hints for the one-handed homemaker, pages 5 to 6, can be used even when your hands are very weak. Deeply grooved teeth grip the cover in the wedge. Support the jar from underneath and extend your wrist to provide enough pressure to turn and loosen the cap.

FIG. 1 To open a waxed cardboard milk container, hold it in both hands, then insert thumbs inside the wedged end. To break the seal, push *all* the way back with both thumbs. If necessary, hold the container with one hand and release the sides of the top with the thumb and fingers of the other hand. Now, pull the center fold all the way forward; then push the sides together to make a spout. If your fingers are very weak, a fork may be used to pry the spout open.

FIG. 2 If peeling and chopping vegetables is a problem, look for convenience foods that are pre-cut and ready-to-use. Onions and green peppers come chopped and frozen in plastic bags. A heated immersible bag can be cut open in a bowl and then picked up from the bottom to empty it. This homemaker has no grasp in her hands but manages to catch the bottom edge of the bag by pressing the thumb of one hand against the fingers of the other.

FIG. 1   FIG. 2

FIG. 3 When grasp is lacking, pouring or sprinkling foods is easier if a container is held in the palm of the hand and supported by the weight of the thumb. Turn your hand over to pour or shake out the contents of the container.

FIG. 4 Occasionally your teeth may come in handy in opening packages made of paper or soft materials that cannot hurt them. Here a tear strip too small to grasp with nonfunctioning fingers is pulled by the teeth.

FIG. 3

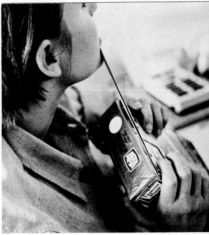

FIG. 4

CUTTING

When you have limited hand and finger function, a knife is usually the most difficult utensil to hold and stabilize. A serrated blade requires less pressure to cut with than a straight-edged knife, as the serrated blade can be used in a sawing motion. Use a board that has two stainless steel nails to stabilize vegetables, fruit, meat, or other items to be cut. (See pages 3 to 4.) Wrapping the knife handle with tape helps make your grasp more secure.

FIGS. 5A & 5B If grasp is totally lacking, the knife can be riveted to a rigid cuff of plastic (Nyloplex or Plexiglas) or metals (such as aluminum) that are molded to fit the hand. The plastics can be cut with a standard wood saw, and heated over a gas flame

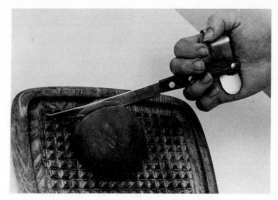

FIG. 5A   FIG. 5B

until flexible enough to mold. Do not have it molded directly over your hand as the plastic will still be hot and may burn your skin.

The knife is attached to the cuff with one or two rivets. If using two, attach only one rivet and try the cuff on your hand. Angle the knife in the most comfortable and efficient position for cutting, and mark the angle. Remove the cuff; drill and insert the second rivet to position it permanently. This device works well for cutting meats, vegetables, and other foods; for spreading butter; and for opening containers, such as cello-wrapped meats and cheeses.

HANDLING EQUIPMENT

FIG. 6 A long-handled utensil, interwoven between your fingers and supported by your thumb, often lets you turn and handle foods without any other assistance. An open broiler eliminates the need to handle doors, pans, or racks, and gives a clear surface for working. (See page 101.)

FIG. 6

FIG. 7 When grasp is lacking, a Universal Cuff may be built up with loops of one-inch-wide elastic to hold frequently used kitchen utensils. The cuff itself is commercially available, or may be constructed as shown on pages 10 and 11.

FIG. 8 If your grasp is very weak, cracking an egg may be accomplished in the following way: First, hold the uncracked egg about 12 inches above an empty bowl. Then, drop the egg so that it falls on its side in the center of the bowl. The shell will crack into two parts. Remove the eggshell by catching it on your thumb, as shown here.

FIG. 9 When lifting a bowl to empty the contents into another pan or dish, stabilize both elbows on the counter for better leverage. Bringing the bowl close to your body while pouring will reduce the weight of lifting. This quadriplegic homemaker

FIG. 7

FIG. 8

FIG. 9

has no grasp in her hands, so she presses them against the sides of the bowl to stabilize it. She holds the rubber scraper in her mouth to scrape out the last of the batter. (Lightweight stainless steel bowls are described on page 215.)

FIG. 10 A person suffering from a loss of hand function resulting from a spinal cord injury may learn to pick up light objects by using tenodesis action. (This means that when the wrist is extended or lifted, the fingers automatically flex in a light, grasping action.) This young homemaker demonstrates tenodesis action as she removes a stick of margarine from its container.

FIG. 10

FIG. 11 If you have complete or very severe loss of grasp, the doctor may recommend an orthosis (an assistive device) to help you perform more activities. A spinal cord injury left this individual with complete loss of hand grasp. However, he does have enough wrist extension to bring his wrist up and hold it in position. This orthosis transfers the extension of

FIG. 11

his wrist to the flexion of his fingers, allowing him to grasp and hold objects.

An orthosis may be very simple, such as one designed to keep your thumb web-space open so that you can grasp things. It may also be more complicated, sometimes involving external power from batteries or gas cylinders. Your physician will tell you if an orthosis might help you, and will refer you, if necessary, to a rehabilitation center that can provide one for you and train you in its use.

Hints for the Homemaker with Arthritis

Household tasks provide light exercise beneficial in keeping the joints limber and muscles active. However, there are ways to avoid strain from overwork, and also simple aids to help you reach or bend.

It's always a good idea to sit down while you work, as prolonged standing puts great stress on the lower extremities and therefore is not recommended. Select a comfortable chair that gives you good back support. If you have arthritis in your upper extremities, you may want a chair with arm supports on which to rest your elbows and forerams. (See the Yield House chair on page 37.) With the addition of a footstool at your feet, such a chair will allow you to work with ease at a standard kitchen counter. When working at a table or drop-leaf counter, you can use a regular kitchen chair. Other aids: a glider chair that can be wheeled around the kitchen, and a wheeled table that cuts down on walking back and forth. (See pages 18, 19 and 121.)

It's also wise to plan your kitchen storage facilities so that all items are placed within reach. A pair of tongs will help you pick up out-of-reach, lightweight items. (See page 48.) If you find it difficult to bend, you can use tongs and a long-handled dustpan and brush. (See pages 48 and 64.) If your reach is limited and you have trouble getting items in and out of the oven, an oven shovel is a handy aid. (See page 182.) If you have difficulty reaching to light a gas stove, try using long barbecue matches. (See page 68.)

Keep your weight down, as too much avoirdupois puts additional stress on arthritic joints. No special diet is prescribed for arthritic patients. Try to keep in the best state of health you possibly can. Eat a balanced diet. The more you enjoy your food and the way it is prepared, the better your appetite will be. (Patients with gout should see their physician for special diet recommendations.)

PROTECTING YOUR HANDS

If you have arthritis in your arms and hands, protect them as much as possible. Avoid tasks requiring great manual strength, such as prying open screw-top jars, or opening cans with a small can opener, or stirring heavy batters. Instead, use a jar opener; an electric or wall can opener; and a lightweight, portable electric mixer. Select lightweight kitchen equipment.

Avoid static or prolonged holding as much as possible. Prop books on a stand while reading. Take breaks from holding vegetables when peeling or cutting them. Stretch or extend your fingers a few times to give them a chance to relax. Set items down rather than holding them. A board with nails for stabilizing (pages 3 to 4) will eliminate the need to hold articles. Use both hands whenever possible. Distributing your efforts between two hands reduces stress on the joints.

Never begin an activity you cannot call a halt to if you are experiencing too much pressure on your hands or other parts of the body.

Try not to carry items. Whenever possible, slide or wheel them from place to place. If you must carry, use a lightweight basket that you can hold over your arm. (See page 121.)

Information on specific exercises and methods of working may be obtained from your physician or the local chapter of The Arthritis Foundation. Sometimes your physician will recommend a resting orthosis, or splint, to hold your hands in a functional position when you're not working. This allows the hands to rest and helps keep the joints in good alignment.

FIG. 1

FIG. 1 To reduce stress on the fingers, use both hands when you work. Here the palms of both hands press down on the knife and help cut a pre-marked butter stick.

FIG. 2 Avoid tasks that place great stress on your hands. Opening jars is one of the most notorious. That extra effort required to release a jar lid may cause trouble.

The Zim Jar Opener grasps the jar lid firmly and holds it as you twist the jar. This device can be used with one hand, although two hands are better since they distribute the effort, thereby lessening stress. Cost is about $3.75 from department stores, or the Zim Manufacturing Company. The opener can be attached to the wall at a location easy to reach, and folds flat against the wall when not in use.

FIG. 3 If you are opening a package that requires a pushing force, such as this waxed cardboard milk container, use the heels of both hands to push back the sides. Do not use your thumbs; they will be forced backward and may stretch the ligaments, causing pain and joint instability.

FIG. 4 A long-handled French chef's knife allows you to distribute work between both hands when cutting or slicing. Keep the point of the knife down on the board to give you better control. The lowered working surface permits your elbows to rest at your sides and gives you a wider working range. This implement is particularly useful when upper extremities are limited in motion.

FIG. 2

FIG. 3

FIG. 4

FIG. 5 Use your strongest joints for an activity. When lifting a pan, for example, do not put weight on the finger joints so that they are forced to the little-finger side of your hand. Instead, use your entire hand and wrist to lift, sliding both hands under the pan. In this way, you transfer the weight from your palms to your wrists and elbows.

FIG. 6 When scrubbing pans, use a sponge that allows you to keep your fingers extended. Because flexion seems more comfortable, we often hold our fingers this way. Then it becomes harder and harder to stretch out our fingers. Any time you have a chance to work with your fingers spread out, by all means do so.

FIG. 5   FIG. 6

GETTING AROUND

FIG. 7 A glider chair with large casters rolls easily and may be used for gathering up food and equipment, and for sitting comfortably while working. Glider chairs are available in a wide price range from hospital equipment firms such as Lumex and Winco. A unit with brakes is recommended, especially if you have poor balance. This one, from Everest and Jennings, costs about $120.

FIG. 8 Your doctor may recommend that you get about in a walker and thereby reduce the stress on your lower extremities. Add a basket to carry foods, dishes, and other items. Baskets are about $4 and up, and are available from hospital-supply firms such as E. F. Brewer and Lumex. This Basklip #105 by Vel-Cor, Inc., has adjustable arms and pivoting clips that can fit a walker or glider. Cost is about $10 and up.

A carry-all with Velcro fastenings attaches over the top rail of the walker. The carry-all is available from Vocational Guidance and Rehabilitation Services for about $5. Trays for walkers are available from Invalex and their distributors.

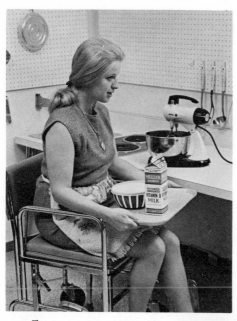

FIG. 7

FIG. 8

HELPFUL REFERENCES

HOME CARE PROGRAMS IN ARTHRITIS—A MANUAL FOR PATIENTS. The
Arthritis Foundation, National Headquarters, 1212 Avenue of the Americas, New York, New York 10036, 1969. Available through your physician or call your local Arthritis chapter.

OSTEOARTHRITIS—HANDBOOK FOR PATIENTS. The Arthritis Foundation,
New York. Free from your local chapter or write to The Arthritis Foundation National Headquarters.

RHEUMATOID ARTHRITIS—HANDBOOK FOR PATIENTS. The Arthritis Foundation, New York. Free from your local chapter or The Arthritis Foundation National Headquarters.

Hints for the Homemaker with Incoordination

Incoordination can be caused by many factors, ranging from weakness associated with chronic illness, to involvement of the nervous
system as in multiple sclerosis, cerebral palsy, and Parkinson's disease. In all of these cases, it's important to keep active and do as
much as you can, including homemaking tasks. This will help you
to function better, stay limber, and even improve your coordination.

There are many aids to help make your mealtime tasks easier.
(See pages 21 to 24.) In some instances, heavier utensils may help
reduce tremors or loss of control. When weakness and poor coordination go together, it's necessary to use implements that are heavy
enough to counteract incoordination or tremors, and yet are light
enough to handle easily.

A word to the woman with multiple sclerosis: your handicap may
quickly fatigue you, so that your incoordination seems to get worse.
If this is the case, learn to do your household work in short shifts.
Also, rely on energy-saving techniques; for instance, slide items instead of lifting them, and use convenience foods and labor-saving
electrical appliances. Prepare meals ahead of time and give yourself
sufficient time to rest up before final preparations.

STABILIZING AND CUTTING

It's important to stabilize the items you are working with. You may
utilize many of the same methods given for the one-handed home-

maker. (See pages 3 to 7.) You may use a specially designed board with stainless steel nails for stabilizing meat, vegetables, and fruit; you'll put a sponge cloth under bowls or pans while mixing; and you'll keep a filled teakettle on the back of the stove, to act as an anchor while stirring or turning food in a pan atop the stove.

Shears will quickly trim meat, if you have good function in one hand. (See page 164.) Large, nonslip handles on knives and other utensils provide a more secure grasp. If the handle has a tendency to slide, wrap it with electrician's tape or spiral it with a rubber band. Make sure that the utensils you use are sturdily constructed, as sudden movements may put more pressure on them than usual.

FIG. 1 Stabilizing one or both arms on a solid surface gives greater control. This homemaker reduces the effect of her incoordination by supporting her arm on the wheelchair rest while pouring.

FIG. 2 This cerebral palsied homemaker rests a vegetable on a large, ordinary sponge to keep the vegetable from sliding while it is being cut. The fork holding the vegetable in place keeps the assisting hand well out of the way of the knife.

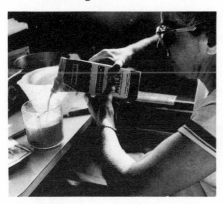 

FIG. 1   FIG. 2

FIG. 3 A serrated knife should be used for cutting and chopping, as the toothed edge provides greater control and is less apt to slip than a straight blade. This knife has sharp, corrugated teeth which permit a slow, steady, sawing motion. To help

FIG. 3

control excess motion while cutting, keep the blade point down on the board. This textured board, designed for use with electric knives, also helps prevent sliding. Cost is about $6 from department stores and mail-order firms, including Maison Michel.

SAFE CARRYING AND AVOIDING SPILLS

FIG. 4 Slide, don't lift; wheel, don't carry. (See pages 37, 38, and 39 of Kitchen Planning to learn how to organize your kitchen

FIG. 4

work area. Also check page 121 for another illustration of a wheeled cart.) Your cart should have a raised rim around the edge, as your movements may occasionally be quick or abrupt. Steel carts are carried by office-supply and hospital-equipment firms, including Lumex, and Everest and Jennings.

FIG. 5 Casseroles and other pans with double handles are excellent for transferring items to and from the oven. This Ekco State Fair Casserole has heat-resistant handles, and costs about $15. The knob is high enough to pick up with a hook grasp.

FIG. 6 This cerebral palsied homemaker sidesteps the chances of spilling a tray of open sandwiches by adding the topping after the sandwiches have been placed on the oven broiler tray. When the sandwiches are ready, she lifts the tray and slides it back under the coils. By holding her arm close to her side, she provides additional control. Measuring liquids is easier if you use large measuring cups to prevent spills.

FIG. 5

FIG. 6

FIG. 7 If you're using a portable, one-handed can opener (Ronson), place a liquid-filled can inside a pan before opening it. Don't try to carry a full can around the kitchen; instead open it near its place of use.

A Zim Jar Opener, set over a small shelf, is handy for opening jars if your grasp is weak. (See pages 16 to 17.) Never install a screw-top opener with only the floor or sink beneath it. The container being opened could accidentally fall and splinter.

FIG. 7

SELECTING UTENSILS

An electric skillet is an excellent appliance for anyone with incoordination. It's stable, cannot tip, comes with single or double handles, and can be used for a variety of purposes. Primarily, it reduces the amount of transferring in and out of the oven, or on and off the stove. Look for a unit with handles you can easily manage, and a control you can turn on without touching the hot metal. A baffle in back of the controls prevents your fingers from touching the metal.

FIG. 8 Although many nonstick, coated pots and pans may be used with regular metal utensils, some require coated or nonmetal kitchen tools. If you have severe loss of coordination, you may find you prefer coated tools for all cooking, since sudden, sharp movements with metal forks or spatulas can mar even fired-on coatings. This nylon fork is part of a six-piece set of heat-resistant and dishwasher-safe tools, including a spatula,

FIG. 8

spoon, ladle, knife, and steel rack. Cost is about $3 per set at houseware stores and mail-order firms, including Suburbia.

Hints for the Homemaker Who Uses a Wheelchair

When using a wheelchair, your chief concern is the design of your kitchen. Getting over to the sink or counter, using the stove, and reaching storage units are all problems.

If your trunk balance is poor, or upper extremities are involved, lifting filled pots to and from a standard work counter or range is difficult. A lowered, drop-in cooking unit is the best solution. If extensive remodeling is not possible, counter-top appliances provide a solution. Table ranges, electric skillets, and broiler-ovens can handle almost every type of cooking. (See pages 83 to 102.)

Jockeying around cabinet and regular doors in a wheelchair is frustrating. So remove the doors! Rearrange storage cabinets to enable you to get one item without having to pick up others. (See pages 44 to 51.)

WHEELCHAIR CONSIDERATIONS

If you are getting a wheelchair, some basic considerations are in order. If you've had one for some time, a few accessories may make it more functional.

A wheelchair cushion increases comfort and, if you are of average or taller height, may also raise you to a height that allows you to use standard-height kitchen equipment. Sitting on a solid seat base is often more comfortable and gives you better trunk balance. A removable rigid seat, cushioned with foam rubber and covered with Naugahyde, is available from Everest and Jennings' distributors.

FIG. 1 Desk arms permit you to come up under a table or lowered counter (29½ inches clearance), and enable you to get close to your work. This is especially helpful if you have poor trunk balance. Desk arms should always be removable so that you can easily transfer to and from the chair. (Malibu Oven, Model 008, by Black Angus, Inc.)

FIG. 1

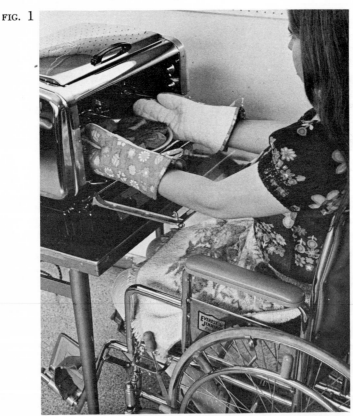

FIG. 2 If the entrance to your kitchen is narrow, or doors (such as the bathroom) cannot be widened enough, a wheelchair-narrower may be the answer. This Narro-Matic unit decreases the width of a folding chair up to 3 inches and can be removed when not needed. Cost is about $40 from hospital-supply firms including Kendall, and Rehabilitation Equipment, Inc.

FIG. 3 When your hands are weak or affected by arthritis, it is easier to wheel the chair if knobs are provided. These projections transfer much of the work of the fingers to the palms of the hands.

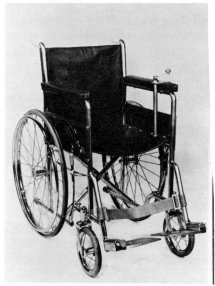
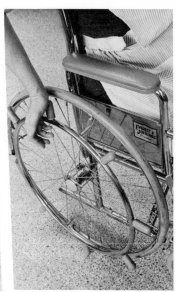

FIG. 2   FIG. 3

FIG. 4 If you have difficulty coming to a standing position but use a wheelchair part of the time, you may consider a hydraulic elevating seat. This seat is pumped up and down by a lever and gives you a rise of 8 inches. It may also allow you to work in a standard-height kitchen when no changes are possible.

Detachable swinging footrests, as shown on this chair, may be either removed or swung out of the way to permit a closer approach to furniture or equipment. When they are completely removed, it's easier to get around narrow hallways.

If your legs should be in a raised position periodically, you may need elevating leg rests. These leg rests should be detachable.

FIG. 5 Unless your kitchen is very small, transporting items around the kitchen is much easier if you use a lapboard. Sometimes the lap tray can substitute for a lowered work surface. It also protects your lap from possible burns in case you spill hot liquids. If you have a wall oven, this lap tray serves as a ready place on which to set hot pans as they come from the oven.

The homemaker pictured here uses her tray as a comfortable mixing surface, and to organize what she needs at the table, and to carry hot things. Metal brackets fit over the chair arms to provide a lowered working surface. This board may be constructed with or without a rim, and can be made of plywood or Masonite. A plan for making it is available from the Occupational Therapy Service, Institute of Rehabilitation Medicine, New York University Medical Center, 400 East 34th Street, New York, New York 10016.

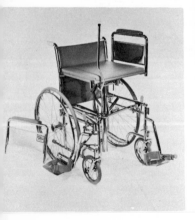

FIG. 4

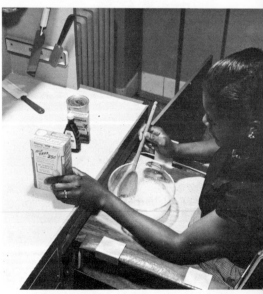

FIG. 5

FIG. 6 This small tray allows you to wheel up to and roll under a lowered work surface. It's placed on the chair by tilting the front up and slipping two hooks under the armrest, and will fit standard Everest and Jennings desk arm wheelchairs. It costs about $14 from Stauffer Wood Products Company.

Other lapboards are also commercially available. However, most have flat rather than lowered surfaces—which is not as good for mixing, cutting, and other kitchen activities. Sources include W. R. Hausmann Woodwork, Inc., Everest and Jennings' distributors, and other hospital houses.

Small objects may be kept at your side in a wheelchair carry-all. Vocational Guidance and Rehabilitation Services makes one in denim with Velcro fastenings that costs about $4. Larger basket units, shown on page 19, are also available.

If you walk with crutches or a cane part of the time, a cane or crutch holder attached to your chair will keep your walking aids within reach.

FIG. 6

NOTE: Only basic wheelchair equipment and accessories have been included here. If you have an extensive physical handicap, your physician and a rehabilitation center will help you arrange for a wheelchair. They will see that you get the proper size, brakes that you can handle, and, if necessary, a special design of chair, including an electrically powered unit for use when upper extremities are very weak.

PUBLICATIONS PROVIDING FURTHER INFORMATION

FUNCTIONAL WHEELS. California State Publication. 50¢ from Department
of General Services, Documents Section, P.O. Box 1612, Sacramento,
California 95807.

SELECTION OF WHEEL CHAIRS. Edward W. Lowman and Howard A.
Rusk. Reprinted from *Postgraduate Medicine*, 1965. A selection of wheelchairs, standard and custom models, measurement charts. Free from Publications Unit, Institute of Rehabilitation Medicine, New York University
Medical Center, 400 East 34th Street, New York, New York 10016.

WHEELCHAIR PRESCRIPTION. Mathew H. M. Lee, Dorothy P. Pezenik,
and Michael M. Dacso. Public Health Service Publication No. 1666,
U.S. Department of Health, Education, and Welfare, Public Health
Service. Available for 20¢ from Superintendent of Documents, U.S.
Government Printing Office, Washington, D.C. 20402.

Hints for the Upper-Extremity Amputee

Learning to use a prosthesis easily and effectively takes time and
practice. Usually, amputees receive training in managing basic controls at a rehabilitation center. Once you have mastered these basics
and know how to position utensils and other items securely, you'll
be able to do many kitchen tasks. Some suggestions are given here,
but also be sure to consult the section on hints for the one-handed
homemaker (pages 2 to 8) for tips on stabilizing food and equipment.

When purchasing kitchen utensils that require the use of both
hands, make sure that you are able to grip the handle comfortably
with either hand. This applies especially to portable mixers, where
you will use one hand to add ingredients while the artificial hand
manages the mixer. Double-handled skillets are easy to lift or
carry, but first check to see that the hook on your prosthesis can
grasp the skillet handle securely.

If you are not using a prosthesis, use the ideas given for the homemaker with one hand. If you have two prostheses, positioning is
even more important; and since lifting is difficult, you may adapt

some of the hints given for the homemaker with weak upper extremities. (See pages 9 to 14.) Be sure to check controls on can openers, mixers, skillets, and other appliances. Consult the section on electricity (pages 70 to 75), as you may find some of the aids for handling plugs helpful.

FIG. 1 When cutting meat or other foods, hold the knife in your good hand; or, if you have two prostheses, in your more dominant device. Position the fork so that the handle rests on the outer surface of the thumb of the hook. Rotate the wrist unit until the tip of the fork rests evenly on the plate surface.

If kitchen utensils tend to slip, you may add another elastic band to your prosthesis, or you can wrap utensil handles with electrician's tape. Flat-handled utensils tend to fit more securely in hooks.

FIG. 2 You may hold a large object by positioning the hook so that the tips face up or down. Secure the object with the rounded part of the hook. A sponge cloth under the jar or object being held will help stabilize it. If it is impossible to exert enough holding force, use a jar opener. (See page 17.)

FIG. 1

FIG. 2

FIG. 3 If you wish to carry a tray or shallow pan, first position the hook fingers so that they are parallel with the tray at waist level. Then grasp the edges of the tray with both hands. Slide the tray edge all the way into the opening of the prosthesis for maximum security. If you have an above-elbow amputation, make sure the prosthetic elbow is locked.

If you are transporting many items, it might be wiser to use a wheeled table to save time and energy. (See pages 120 to 121.)

FIG. 4 When washing dishes, hold the dish in your good hand and the scrubbing mop or sponge in your prosthesis. Avoid detergents, as they tend to dissolve lubricating oils in the hook and wrist mechanism of your artificial limb. If you wash dishes often, make sure to clean and oil the threads and bearing of the hook frequently.

FIG. 3   FIG. 4

Hints for the Homemaker with Loss of Sensation

There are several simple precautions to take in the kitchen if you have loss of sensation in your hands or other parts of your body due to a spinal cord lesion or a neurological involvement such as multiple sclerosis or the severing of a nerve. Some suggestions are listed on the next page.

Always use asbestos-padded potholders when handling a hot pan. Whenever possible, slide pans instead of lifting them to prevent spilling.

When working at the stove, select kitchen tools that have non-heat-conducting handles. When you use an ordinary spoon or fork to stir hot foods, the metal can quickly heat up without your feeling it.

Ladle hot liquids to prevent spills. Remove other hot foods with a slotted spoon, instead of lifting the pot to drain or pour.

Use thermometers to help you determine when a correct heat is reached. A thermospoon, commercially available at department stores or from Gaydell, Inc., indicates cooking and serving temperatures up to 450° on an easy-to-read dial at the top of the handle. This unit is dishwasher-safe and has no glass to break. Cost is about $6.

If you're in a wheelchair, use a small lapboard (preferably with a slightly raised rim) to carry hot pans and casseroles. Don't put the items in your lap! (See page 28 to 29)

When cutting meats or vegetables, use a breadboard with two stainless steel nails. (See page 3.) This device will stabilize the food and also keep your fingers out of the way.

Select knives and other utensils with large handles so that they can be grasped more securely.

When working at the kitchen sink, you may find that the hot water faucet overheats to such a degree that when you touch the handle it burns you. To avoid this, have someone check on the faucet handle for you. If the handle habitually gets too hot, install a faucet turning aid to protect your hands. (See page 132.)

Get a dishwasher, if you can afford one. It's a great convenience and safety aid. Otherwise, when you do dishes, be sure to wear insulated rubber gloves, such as the Bluettes made by Pioneer Rubber Co. (See page 131.)

Hints for the Homemaker with Limited Vision

The following suggestions are for those of you who have limited vision and find it difficult to handle mealtime tasks or to read small

print or temperature controls. If you have marked loss of vision, you
may obtain help and training from local organizations for the blind,
and from national groups such as the American Foundation for
the Blind or the National Society for the Prevention of Blindness.

Your kitchen should be carefully organized to promote safety and
ease in working. Eliminate protuberances you may bump into, or
small rugs you may trip on. Plan a specific place for everything, and
store together tools used at the same time. Put knives in a safe holder
that will cover the blades. (See page 58.) Pull-out shelves or Lazy
Susans reduce the hazard of reaching for hard-to-see items in the
back of dark cabinets. Equip cabinets with sliding doors instead
of swinging ones, to prevent head-on collisions.

Brightly colored tape should be used to mark Off positions on
temperature controls; this will enable you to make sure that your
appliances are completely turned off when not in use. If controls are
difficult to match with the burners on the stove, use four colors of
tape, coding each burner to its control knob. If you have a hood
over your range, rim it with a band of brightly colored tape to avoid
accidentally hitting it.

When vision is impaired in any way, touch and position senses are
affected. When peeling or cutting foods, use a board with two stainless steel nails. (See page 3.) This will stabilize the food and keep
your fingers out of the way.

Potholders should be asbestos-padded, and pot handles should be of
non-heat-conducting material. Baking pans with handles provide a
surer grip and help reduce the danger of burns. Look for measuring
cups with large printing. (See page 160.)

The American Foundation for the Blind distributes several helpful aids. Their free catalog, *Aids and Appliances*, lists all kinds of
homemaking equipment, including an immersible electric frypan
having a heat control with raised markings, and several dry and liquid
measuring implements.

Large-print cookbooks for the partially sighted are now available.
The Campbell Soup Company distributes a free, large-type, paperback book that gives recipes and ideas for the use of convenience
foods. To obtain a copy, write for *A Campbell Cookbook: Easy Ways
to Delicious Meals*, Large Type Edition, Volunteers Service for the
Blind, 332 South 13th Street, Philadelphia, Pennsylvania 19107.

General Mills also publishes a large type cookbook and recorded cooking lessons. Write to General Mills, Inc., Betty Crocker Kitchens, 9200 Wayzata Boulevard, Minneapolis, Minnesota 55426. *The New York Times Large Type Cookbook* by Jean Hewett, Golden Press, New York, 1968, gives over 300 recipes in large, clear print.

FIG. 1 This is the size of the print in *The New York Times Large Type Cookbook*. Price is $9.95 at local bookstores.

FIG. 2 If impaired vision makes it difficult for you to read recipes printed in small type, you might try using a magnifying glass that rests on the book and enlarges the type. Various sizes and kinds of magnifiers are carried by opticians and department stores. This rectangular reader is made by Bausch and Lomb.

Cornish Hens Hawaiienne

Yield: 6 servings 1554372

6 Rock Cornish hens

½ cup butter

1 teaspoon salt

¼ teaspoon black pepper

FIG. 1

FIG. 2

FIG. 3

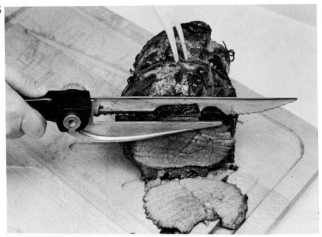

FIG. 3 This Adjusta-Knife, by General Slicing Machine Company, has a guide that is set to determine the thickness of the slice (up to ⅝ inch). As the serrated knife blade cuts through, the guide rests against the outer edge of the food, providing even slices. The width of the slice can be determined by feeling the space between the top of the knife and the guide edge. Price is about $7 at department stores and from the American Foundation for the Blind.

Kitchen Planning

The kitchen is your main arena in caring for your family. When a physical disability or age slows you down, or affects your ability to work, or reduces your energy, then it's time to remodel your kitchen to meet your needs.

In planning alterations, first make a floor plan of the kitchen as it is; next, list the problems you have in handling appliances or working in kitchen areas. Use this list when you plan changes. Before embarking on major remodeling, talk to a contractor or architect about problems you may encounter in altering the height of drain pipes or in changing wiring. At the end of this chapter are a few publications which will help you design the best possible arrangement, and also assist you in choosing the equipment you need.

A few examples are given here to start you thinking.

SITTING TO WORK

One of the basic ways to conserve energy in the kitchen is to sit in a comfortable chair while you work. Select a chair that gives you proper support. You'll need a chair of standard height to work at a kitchen table, and a higher chair at a sink or work counter. When using the higher chair, put a box or stool under your feet for proper support.

FIG. 1 This Admiral's chair has a large, contoured swivel seat and full, curved arms for support and comfort. It comes in two seat heights, of 24 and 30 inches. The wheeled table provides an extra work counter. When the homemaker wants to use the sink, she pushes the wheeled table out of the way and swivels her chair around to the sink. A simple, wooden footstool supports her feet as she works.

FIG. 1

The Admiral's chair has widespread, hardwood legs that can be cut off at the turnings if a specific height is needed. Cost is about $22 unfinished and $32 finished, plus shipping. A similar Captain's chair comes with half arms, for $12 or $17, depending on whether it's finished or not. Both are available from Yield House.

Wheeled tables can be purchased at department stores and office-supply stores, including Sears Roebuck, for about $7 and up. (See pages 120 to 121.)

The footstool may be necessary if you have weakness or arthritis in the lower extremities. Keep your feet flat on the stool with the ankles at right angles to give you greater ease. A long dowel or broomstick handle may be attached to the side of the stool to enable you to adjust it under your feet or move it when you change your position in the chair. Instructions for making this stool are available at the Homemaking Unit, Occupational Therapy Service, Institute of Rehabilitation Medicine, New York University Medical Center, 400 East 34th Street, New York, New York 10016.

If you are working from a wheelchair, or seated on a high stool, it's easier to use the sink when the cupboard doors and molding have been removed. This is an inexpensive process that permits you to work with greater comfort.

WORKING FROM A WHEELCHAIR

If you are using a wheelchair or have marked loss of power in your upper extremities, careful kitchen planning will help you carry out mealtime tasks more easily.

Work surfaces should be the proper height to allow for wheelchair clearance. This means that counter tops should be about 31 inches high and have 29½ inches clearance from the floor to permit wheelchair arms to slide under the counter. Also, the area under the counter should be open, to allow you to move your feet around. A continuous counter, from refrigerator to sink to range, will permit you to slide items instead of having to carry them.

If you must cook from a wheelchair but are unable to lower kitchen work surfaces, it's almost always possible to add a lower work area. A standard kitchen table of proper height may be used, or a drop-leaf table can be attached to a vacant wall. Sears Roebuck, Miles Kimball, and department stores carry drop-leaf tables complete with fittings for about $3.50 and up. Make sure the supports under the drop-leaf are sturdy enough to take the combined weight of the tabletop, your own arms while working, and the weight of your cooking utensils.

If you have good use of your upper extremities, you can often use a standard-height range, even if you are working in a wheelchair or a glider chair. Use pans with sides that are high enough to prevent spilling, yet are low enough to permit you to see into the pan to check your cooking progress. A small mirror on a handle may be helpful; you can tuck it into the wheelchair beside you. A large mirror placed over the range top gets greasy and steamed up, so that it's hard to see, and hard to reach and clean.

FIG. 2A This kitchen was especially designed for a person in a wheelchair. The undersurface of the counter just clears the wheelchair arms, thus allowing the homemaker to get close to her work. (An undersurface height of 29½ inches is needed to accommodate the standard wheelchair.) A pull-out board to the right of the sink serves as a resting place for items from the refrigerator. Storage shelves at the back of the counter hold items frequently used.

The stainless steel sink is 5½ inches deep, and has been designed with a rear well for a disposal unit so that the drain pipe does not interfere with knee room. It measures 22 inches wide and 16 inches deep. This Waste-All sink is from Elkay Manufacturing Company.

The vertical files shown here were custom-made, with adjustable boards that can be rearranged. If you wish to design your own vertical storage at home, merely cut sheets of Masonite or thin plywood to size. Space them to accommodate your pans, and attach them along the shelf area with brads. Frequently, vertical shelving can be added below existing cabinets

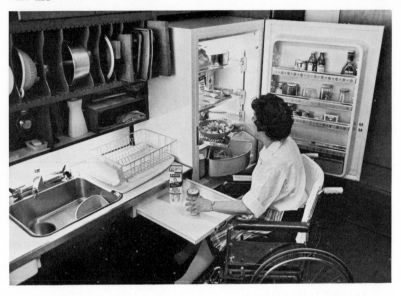

for the use of the homemaker in a wheelchair. Upper cabinets are kept for less frequently used items, which another member of the family can get down when required.

FIG. 2B This homemaker uses an electric wall oven and counter-top electric cooking surface. The oven is by Frigidaire, the cooking top by Thermador. When selecting appliances, be sure to check several manufacturers, as models differ widely.

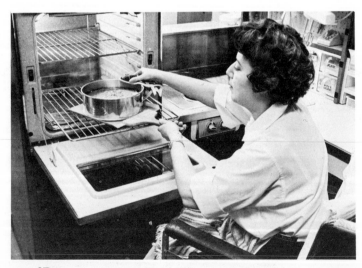

FIG. 3A This homemaker lives in a low-rent housing project, and, with the help of the kitchen planning consultant at a rehabilitation center, she was able to make basic changes that would allow her to function efficiently from her wheelchair. The sink could not be changed, due to the plumbing. However, under-sink space was opened up for leg room, enabling her to use it for washing dishes and cleaning foods. A drop-leaf table serves as a work area. Since others in the family use this compact kitchen, the table folds down when not in use.

FIG. 3B A 36-inch gas range was too high for her to manage from a wheelchair. Instead a gas stack-on cooking top was placed on a low cabinet; it provides safe, convenient cooking. Although gas stack-on tops are harder to find than electric, they are available from several manufacturers. Check to see that they are shallow enough to set at wheelchair counter height and permit you to get your foot pedals close up or underneath.

FIG. 3C A stack-on gas oven with a pull-out broiler is easy to handle from the wheelchair. The door opens 26 inches from the floor.

FIG. 3A   FIG. 3B

FIG. 3C

FIG. 4 When you are confined to a wheelchair, and it is not possible to remodel the kitchen to permit you to work comfortably at the sink, it's a good idea to keep a water container in a convenient place. This 6-quart capacity plastic container provides enough water for most cooking, and can be refilled by family members as needed. A small shelf over a counter, or drop-leaf table, provides a place where you can set the pan or measuring cup to catch the water. The dripless spout releases water when a rubber button on the front of the unit is depressed. Cost is about $2 and up from mail-order firms and department stores. Similar units cost up to $7.

FIG. 5 Push-button controls are easier to handle than knobs when your hand function is impaired by weakness or poor coordination. This unit is by General Electric.

FIG. 4

FIG. 5

LIGHTING

Proper lighting increases safety and prevents eyestrain. When install-
ing a new work space, or rearranging your present area, additional
lighting may be necessary. Various types of fixtures are available
from electrical supply stores and mail-order firms, including Sears
Roebuck and Montgomery Ward.

FIG. 6

FIG. 6 This "Little Inch" light, by Alkco Manufacturing Company, can
be installed under a wall cabinet and provides direct light on
your working surface. It is only 1 inch deep and gives off a
soft, unobtrusive light. It comes with a push-type or toggle
switch. A built-in grounded convenience outlet accommodates portable kitchen appliances, and a 6-foot cord plugs
into a wall outlet. The unit shown here is 12½ inches long,
and costs about $6. Other sizes are 21¼, 24½, and 42½
inches long. Alkco fixtures are carried by department stores
and mail-order firms.

Pegboard shelf brackets provide extra storage space in the
kitchen and other parts of the house. Look for brackets that
have a supporting triangular underpiece. These 8-inch-long
shelf brackets, by Masonite Corporation and Kerr Wire Products Company, fit a ⅛-inch or ¼-inch pegboard and cost
about 50¢ per pair from hardware stores.

FURTHER HELP

If no money is available for kitchen changes, you may qualify
for assistance under the State Division of the Vocational Rehabili-

tation program. Homemaking is considered a remunerative occupation. Retraining can include counseling, diagnostic and physical restorative services, and tools or equipment to enable you to carry on homemaking. Equipment includes kitchen changes—both material and labor costs.

PUBLICATIONS PROVIDING FURTHER INFORMATION

PLANNING KITCHENS FOR HANDICAPPED HOMEMAKERS. Virginia Hart Wheeler.

This book gives step-by-step details for remodeling kitchens to meet the needs of persons with various handicaps. Although written for the rehabilitation professional, the ideas and directions are clear enough for you to follow. Price is $2 from the Publications Unit, Institute of Rehabilitation Medicine, New York University Medical Center, 400 East 34th Street, New York, New York 10016. Ask for Rehabilitation Monograph XXVII.

KITCHENS FOR WOMEN IN WHEELCHAIRS. Circular 841, Helen E. McCullough and Mary B. Farnham, College of Agriculture, University of Illinois, Urbana, Illinois, 1961. Cost is 50¢.

Kitchen Storage

Full use of available storage space is always important, even more so when your reach is limited or your hand function is impaired, making it difficult for you to pick up items from a shelf. The homemaker with the use of one hand finds it frustrating to have to lift many items out of the way to reach a single container at the back of a shelf. The person with weak grasp or poor coordination wants to reach one item without knocking down others.

Plan your kitchen storage to fit your physical and your cooking needs. Items should be arranged so that you can easily reach objects that are often used. This may mean that you have to store items commonly kept on top shelves nearer to the bottom so that you can get at them quickly. Organize your storage to suit the kind of meals you prepare. If you use many convenience foods, store them within easy reach. If you rely heavily on portable appliances, keep them at the back of the counter space permanently, or on a table ready for use. For instance, if you need your electric skillet for almost every meal, why bother putting it away when you'll only have to take it out again?

The first step in planning kitchen storage is to organize.

Look at each work area in your kitchen. Which items are most frequently used? Which items do you constantly have to take out and put away again? Would it be better to keep these out all the time? Which items don't you use at all? These can be stored in a relatively inaccessible place. Are there some items, like measuring cups or spoons and knives, that you keep moving from place to place? It might be better to have duplicates at both the sink and mixing center.

See where you can add storage aids, such as pegboard panels, wall hooks, open shelves, and cabinet organizers. A few simple fixtures, strategically placed, will expand the capacity of space accessible to you. Do you have a closet that's not being used to full advantage? What about adding pull-out shelves and pegboard sides? Do you have any empty wall space where you might put narrow shelving to store canned food and other items? How about building a storage unit on the back of a door? You can buy adjustable shelves; they're manufactured by S. A. Hirsh.

When deciding on storage units, select ones that allow you to pre-position all utensils so you can easily grasp them.

Put the items you use most often in your work area. Keep heavier items where they can be slid back and forth. Store lightweight objects, such as baskets or plastic food containers, higher up. Keep a reaching device handy to retrieve fallen objects or to get things off high shelves.

Major kitchen reorganization has already been discussed under Kitchen Planning. (See pages 36 to 45.) The items shown here are merely a sample of small units you may wish to add to your kitchen. Many ingenious storage ideas can be found in popular magazines such as *American Home, Better Homes and Gardens, Family Circle, Good Housekeeping, House and Garden, House Beautiful, Popular Mechanics, Sunset Magazine,* and *Woman's Day.*

BACK-OF-COUNTER STORAGE

FIG. 1 Lightweight, plastic, slide-out canisters will store commonly used foods near at hand. These units, made in Norway, come in several styles and sizes, and are available at culinary stores, including Norsk. The ones shown here cost $27 and up. Other manufacturers' models start at about $8 and up.

FIG. 2 A Lazy Susan at the back of a work counter utilizes unused space and puts frequently used foods within easy reach. This Rubbermaid Twin Turntable (Model B1-2937) is 10½ inches in diameter and 5¾ inches high, and costs about $2.

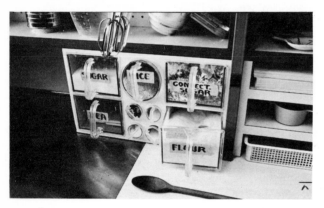

FIG. 1

FIG. 2

FIG. 3 This pan and tray storage rack (No. 218), by Grayline Housewares, Inc., holds pans, cutting boards, baking sheets, skillets, pot covers, and pie plates within easy reach. It may be placed in a cabinet, in a deep drawer to provide vertical storage, or at the back of a counter. The vinyl-coated rack measures 11¾ by 7¾ inches and costs about $2.50 to $3.

FIG. 4 Handy-Dandy plastic caps snap into a ⅛-inch pegboard to hold quarter-turn glass jars, like those in which baby foods come. Secured by a double bracket, these jars may be turned with one hand, and are useful for spices and herbs. Cost is about $1 for 10, from Wickcliffe Industries, Inc.

FIG. 5 This homemaker relies on a low Lazy Susan to hold most of her basic food supplies. Here, she uses a cookie sheet to carry everything to one place for baking. Each item should be stored so that you can retrieve it with one hand without lifting other objects out of the way. This sometimes calls for cutting down on the number of utensils you use. Lazy Susan cabinets may be purchased in standard sizes from companies, including Long Bell, and Sears Roebuck, or may be custom-built.

FIG. 3

FIG. 4

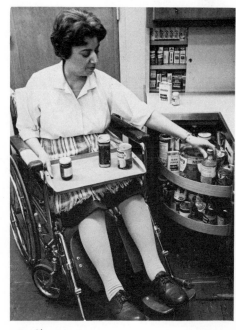

FIG. 5

FIG. 6 Lightweight items, like baskets, may be kept on higher shelves where you can reach them with a pair of tongs. When bending is difficult, long-handled tongs help reach pans and other items stored down low. Attach these tongs to your wheelchair with a short dog leash to keep them handy. These 18-inch-long scissor tongs are available from houseware stores for about $1. Manufacturers include Ekco, and John Clark Brown.

FIG. 6

FIG. 7 A pull-out rack for pots and pans, installed in a cabinet or under a counter top, eliminates stacking; it also makes it easier to remove a single pot with one good or two weak hands without bending. The slide-out rack, 18 inches long, holds eight pans, and costs $2.50 up from hardware and houseware stores, and mail-order firms. Manufacturers include Knape and Vogt, and Grayline Housewares, Inc.

FIG. 7

FIG. 8 This standard undercounter cabinet has been reorganized with a Rubbermaid Storage Turntable (FO-2302, 19 x 21 inches, or FO-2300, 15¾ inches diameter) and a turntable bin (FO-2303). The Rubbermaid Slide-Out Storage Drawer is attached to the top half shelf. It comes in a standard 19½-inch depth, with four widths: 9, 12, 14, or 16 inches.

FIG. 8

FIG. 9 Vertical drawer dividers eliminate stacking, making it easier to remove desired items. Bread drawers or deep-base drawers may be efficiently converted with Masonite, or ⅛- to ¼-inch wood separators, cut to size and fitted with metal brad holders.

FIG. 9

FIG. 10 Extra shelves can be built at home from a variety of materials. Shelf extenders are also commercially available from several sources. This vinyl-coated Adjustable Stack-A-Shelf (Model No. 712), by Grayline Housewares, Inc., extends from 18 to 32 inches, and can be stacked. Size is 16¾ inches long, 5½ inches high, and 9 inches wide. Cost is about $4.

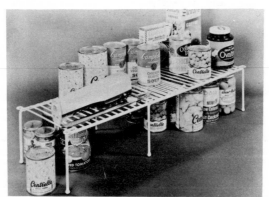

FIG. 10

REFRIGERATOR STORAGE

Refrigerator storage should be organized to make it as easy as possible for you to get things in and out, especially when you have limited use of your hands, or difficulty in reaching. Lazy Susan units, such as those by Rubbermaid, hold a variety of small containers that may be brought to the front of the shelf for accessibility.

When using a wheelchair, refrigerator door shelves should be well utilized. If your grasp is weak, position your wheeled table or lapboard as close to the refrigerator as possible for quick transfer of items. Store heavier units on a shelf even with the surface so you can slide them to and from the refrigerator. An extra shelf in the freezer often does away with the need to lift one item to reach another. A 10½- by 10-inch rack costs about $1.20 from variety stores and mail-order firms.

Storing Food

Storing food correctly is vital to its taste and freshness, and necessary to preserve its vitamin content. Some food stored in the refrigerator should be wrapped or covered to prevent loss of moisture, while other food, such as fresh meat, should be loosely wrapped. Freezer wrappings should always be airtight so that the food will not dry out or become freezer-burned.

Acquaint yourself with the variety of food wraps carried by your local supermarkets. These include aluminum foil, plastic bags and wraps, waxed paper, and freezer paper. Watch for hints on how to use them to reduce your preparation and clean-up time. You'll find some ideas in the section on Handy Tricks with Food Wraps. (See pages 53 to 55.)

FOOD WRAPS AND STORAGE CONTAINERS

Plastic bags are useful for freezer, refrigerator, or dry storage. They come in a variety of sizes with twist-tie closures. Some stores also carry a jumbo size (18 x 24 inches), which is practical for storing a big roast or large amounts of fruit, vegetables, and greens. Extra strong, double-walled, quilted plastic bags are particularly good for freezer storage. These come with twist-tie closures in 1-quart and 1-gallon sizes.

You can also buy large plastic garbage bags to line waste-disposal cans.

Aluminum foil wraps are practical for the freezer since you can press foil around the food and exclude air. For freezer storage, buy heavy-duty or super-strength foil (available in two popular widths of 12 and 18 inches). The length of the rolls varies from 25 to about 200 feet.

Plastic wraps are useful for wrapping foods for refrigerator storage (available in 12-inch and 18-inch widths and in lengths of 50 and 100 feet).

Storage containers with tight-fitting lids are available in flexible plastic, rigid plastic, and glass. They can be used for freezer, refrigerator, and dry storage. Store 'n See Pyrex ware, which are round containers with white or avocado-colored lids, can be used as attractive counter canisters or for storing food in your refrigerator.

Tupperware makes round refrigerator containers called Small Wonderliers. These come in sets that include 1, 2, and 4-cup sizes. The lids have tabs for easier opening. Tupperware also makes small refrigerator bowls for leftovers, and special large containers for ice cream, cake, pie, a loaf of bread, and salad. (Available only on the home party plan. Look for your dealer in the yellow pages of the phone book under Housewares.)

Other freezer containers of flexible plastic also work well for refrigerator storage. They come in a variety of shapes and sizes including 1 pint, 1 quart, and 2 quarts, and are made by Republic Molding, Deka Plastics, and others. Cost is 30¢ and up for each container. When plastic tops are hard to remove because of arthritis or weakness in the hands, try using the blunt end of a bottle-cap opener.

Foil pans for baking, roasting, or freezing are available in a variety of sizes and shapes including potato shells, pie plates, loaf pans, square and round cake pans, small angel cake pans, and one-piece broilers.

Paper and foil muffin-pan liners come in several sizes. Use them instead of greasing pans when you are making muffins or cupcakes . . . there's no clean-up. (Also see PAM on page 135.)

Paper plates and cups are acceptable nowadays for casual family meals and even for company. You can buy handsome woven bamboo plate-holders to stabilize paper plates and make them look festive.

PROPER STORAGE OF FRESH FOOD

Store *fresh meat* in the coldest part of the refrigerator. It should be loosely wrapped in waxed paper or aluminum foil. Meat should not be washed before storage since a damp surface is undesirable. Variety meats and ground meats are more perishable than other meats and should be cooked within one or two days if not frozen.

Cured and smoked meats, sausage, and ready-to-serve meats should be stored in the refrigerator in their original wrappings.

Leftover cooked meats should be cooled promptly, covered or wrapped to prevent drying, and stored in the refrigerator.

Green vegetables, including leafy greens, should be stored in the vegetable crisper or in plastic bags in the refrigerator. Use them as quickly as possible.

Store *ripe fruits* such as apples, peaches, cherries, grapes, pears, and plums in a covered container or in perforated plastic bags on the refrigerator shelf.

Citrus fruits, bananas, uncut melons, avocados, and pineapples are best stored at cool room temperature

Berries should be kept dry and refrigerated until ready to use. (Do not wash until serving time.)

Fresh dairy products should be kept tightly covered in the refrigerator.

HANDY TRICKS WITH FOOD WRAPS

Freeze ground meat in patties. Place two pieces of foil or waxed paper between each serving for easy separation later. Meat stored as patties thaws more rapidly.

If meat or pastry starts to get too brown while roasting or baking, cover with foil.

Store foods that absorb odors in tightly closed plastic bags.

Keep lettuce crisp longer by wrapping in damp paper toweling and putting it in a plastic bag in the refrigerator.

Marinate meat in a plastic bag. Squeezing or shifting the bag's position in the bowl will turn the meat so that it marinates evenly.

Store brown sugar in a plastic bag to keep it soft.

Roll pie crust between sheets of waxed paper. This way you can judge the size more easily, and picking it up with one hand is a cinch.

To provide yourself with ready-prepared main dishes, make double portions of casseroles. Freeze the extra portion in a casserole dish lined with foil, then remove the foil-wrapped portion from the dish. When ready to use, put the frozen contents back in the casserole to thaw and bake.

Line your broiler pan with foil to reduce scrubbing. Do not cover broiler racks unless you make holes in the foil to allow the fat to drop through to a pan below.

When your grasp is weak or lacking in both hands, you may find the easiest way to handle food wraps is to put the box on the counter in front of you and pull out the needed amount by holding it between both hands and shaking gently, or grasping the wrap edge in your mouth and pulling the box down. To tear off, press wrap down with your forearm along the edge of the box.

Alcoa Wrap is now distributing pre-folded sheets of aluminum foil that eliminate the need for tearing.

FIG. 1 Wall-hanging wrap holders are practical, particularly if you have the use of only one hand. Holders in designs and colors to match your kitchen are available at department stores. For efficient use of several wraps, try a three-tiered unit, such as this one by Rubbermaid. Cost of this unit is about $8.

FIG. 1

Matching plastic drawers, also by Rubbermaid, install under cabinets for convenient storage of dry foods. Drawers tilt down to use.

FIG. 2A This Seal-A-Meal unit, by Dazey Products Company, allows you to fill your own immersible bags for refrigerator or freezer storage. You can make double amounts of a main dish or dessert, and freeze them until needed. The second go-round there's no preparation or pots to clean. Leftover meats and sauces can be put together and kept for another meal. Foods like rice or breaded meats don't get soggy when reheated. An E-Z Fill rigid plastic ring fits inside the top of the bag and holds it open. Persons with weak hands or the use of only one hand can prop the stiff, plastic bag against the side of a box or bowl to keep it upright while filling.

FIG. 2A   FIG. 2B

FIG. 2B Once filled, the plastic ring is lifted out, the bag slipped on two pegs, and the top of the base is pressed down lightly to heat-seal the bag. This unit can be wall-mounted; if, however, you have hand trouble it's easier to work at a counter. Cost is about $20 with an assortment of bags of various sizes. More bags can be ordered by mail or are available from Seal-A-Meal dealers. A similar unit, Meals-In-Minutes, is available from Sears Roebuck (Catalog No. 34 A-6555) for about $18.

Selecting Kitchen Tools

Choosing the proper equipment will help you to overcome difficulties posed by a physical disability or limited mobility, and will enable you to function more efficiently in your kitchen. This book gives suggestions for selecting or adapting equipment for many phases of food preparation. You will notice that certain basics apply to every tool or item you use.

Is it versatile? Can the item fill more than one need? A good knife with a sharp, medium-length blade (8 to 10 inches long) and a comfortable handle can perform many cutting tasks. A hand brush can scrub vegetables and fruits, and dishes. An ovenproof, stoveproof casserole with good handles is a safe utensil for cooking on the stove, baking in the oven, and serving at the table. The fewer utensils and pieces of equipment you use, the less space they take to store, and the handier they are when you need them.

Is it durable? The item should be well made. Make sure that handles have sturdy attachments so that they will not become wobbly and unsafe. Mechanical aids should perform without frequent adjustments or repairs. Buy reliable brands to assure quality. All items used at the stove should be heatproof.

Is it easy to clean? The design of the utensil should be smooth. Avoid decorative grooves that require extra scrubbing time. Nonstick interior and baked-on exterior finishes on pans and utensils are easier to care for.

Is it suitably priced? Seek the maximum quality in the item that works best for you. Money doesn't always determine quality, but sometimes it is necessary to pay more for an item of superior quality.

KNIVES

Knives are probably the most frequently used kitchen tools today, because almost every meal requires some cutting preparation. Although there are many excellent knives on the market, you may find that you prefer two or three basic knives because of limited manual ability. For example, you may find yourself relying on a utility knife, a French chef's knife, and perhaps a roast or meat slicer.

When buying a knife, check to see how it feels in your hand. Is it balanced and comfortable to hold? You don't want a knife that's too heavy. On the other hand, you need one that's sturdily constructed, with the handle firmly attached to the blade. At least a third of the length of the blade should extend into the handle, and be secured by two or more rivets. When your grasp is impaired, a larger handle is easier to hold. Shaped handles are also easier to grip.

In general, sharp knives are safer than dull ones. A sharp knife will slice smoothly, while a dull one requires more pressure and may slip while you're cutting. Serrated blades allow more control.

Electric can openers often come with accessory sharpeners. If you are working with one hand, or with two weak ones, make sure the unit automatically turns on when you apply pressure, or that it has an On-Off switch. Some models require you to push a button down while holding the knife in the other hand. It's preferable to choose a device that can be operated with one hand. For example, the sharpener on the General Electric Universal electric can opener has a lever that locks in place and permits the motor to continue running. (See page 79.)

FIG. 1 Small hand sharpeners may be attached to the wall or the side of a cabinet. However, this Vacu-Base knife sharpener from the General Slicing Machine Co. doesn't need to be attached; suction action permits it to adhere to a nonporous counter or tabletop. The small lever controls the suction. Cost is about $1.50 from houseware stores.

.FIG. 1

STORAGE

Make sure that knives are carefully stored so that you are protected from blades when you reach for other objects.

FIG. 2 Install the Knife-Pal in a convenient corner or at the side of a kitchen drawer so that your favorite knife is ready for use. The blade is completely protected; thus, when you reach for other utensils in a drawer, you will not accidentally cut yourself. The adhesive mounting attaches securely to wood or steel. The knife is inserted at an angle, making the handle easier to grasp. Cost is about $1.25, plus 50¢ postage from the Window-Pal Company.

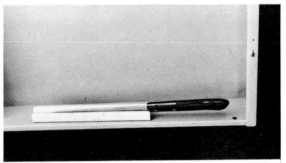

FIG. 2

FIG. 3 This coiled wire unit holds knives in a horizontal position with the blades facing down. The handles are easy to grasp. The unit is attached to the bottom of a drawer. Cost is about

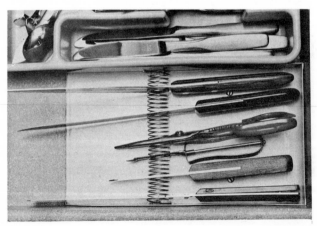

FIG. 3

$2 from department stores. Other storage units which hang on the wall are available from department stores and mail-order firms for about $1.50 and up.

Hints for Using Knives

Let roasts stand for 15 to 20 minutes before carving. The meat is firmer and easier to slice when it cools off. Cut meats across the grain to break up the long muscle fibers, making it easier to chew.

Cut cakes or breads with a gentle sawing motion. A scalloped knife used this way will not tear delicate textures.

To protect fine edges and prevent accidents, wash, rinse, and dry knives immediately after using them. Do not soak them.

Always use the knife on a cutting board to protect the blade as well as other surfaces.

GRATING AND MINCING

FIG. 4 With most recipes that call for minced or grated foods, you can usually find a prepared product, like instant minced onions, frozen chopped chives and parsley, and freeze-dried orange or lemon rind.

There are times, however, when the item called for in the recipe is not available in a ready-to-use form, or when you want the additional flavor that freshly minced or grated food provides. For example, nothing can rival fresh lemon peel.

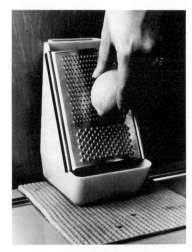

FIG. 4

This Swedish-designed hand grater comes with a plastic base. It has three stainless steel grating and slicing rasps, graded from very fine to coarser slicing levels. The slanted surface is convenient to use, and, if you are using one hand, you can back the unit against a counter ledge, and stabilize it on a sponge cloth. Cost is about $4.50 from culinary specialty shops, department stores, and mail-order firms such as La Cuisiniere and The Krebs.

APRONS

Protecting yourself against spills and splatters while you work in the kitchen is only good common sense. When selecting an apron to be worn near a hot stove, make sure that the material is not flammable. Do *not* use plastic or synthetics like nylon. Instead choose cloth or rubber. The aprons shown here all have special features that make them attractive to homemakers.

FIG. 5 Apron hoops eliminate the need to tie sashes or bows. This is particularly useful if only one hand is functioning, or if your range of motion is limited due to weakness or arthritis. Plastic waist hoops are available for under $1 from the notions' departments of most large stores, or mail-order firms, including Rehab Aids and Cleo Living Aids. They come in three sizes: small, medium, and large.

Aprons to fit the hoops may be made from terrycloth towels. One end is folded over to make a casing for the hoop. Large bath towels may be cut in half to make two aprons; both raw edges are turned over as casings. Terrycloth is absorbent, attractive, and easy to launder. If you wish, you can use smaller towels and fold them up at the bottom to provide large pockets.

FIG. 5

FIG. 6 A plastic apron hoop keeps this vinyl lap tray securely in place. The raised rim makes it helpful to carry foods and other items while in a wheelchair. The tray comes with a solid insert so that it may be used for mixing or other activities requiring a firm surface. The insert may be removed to provide a more flexible surface. The tray is low enough to permit a close approach to counters and tables of wheelchair height. Cost is about $9 from Vocational Guidance and Rehabilitation Services, or self-help equipment firms, including Cleo Living Aids.

FIG. 7 This Carry-All Apron has a full bib for protection. A concealed elastic provides an adjustable waistband. The deep pockets are terrycloth-backed and plastic-lined for carrying damp cleaning cloths, sponges, and other items around the house. The apron comes in aqua, yellow, or pink seersucker, in two sizes: medium for a 29- to 32-inch waistline, and large for a 32- to 35-inch waistline. Larger or smaller sizes can be made to order. Cost is about $6.50 from Vocational Guidance and Rehabilitation Services.

FIG. 6

FIG. 7

HANDLING RECIPES

FIG. 8 A simple book stand will enable you to read a cookbook more easily and will protect the book from food splatters and spills. This adjustable book rest can be angled for comfortable viewing, and folds flat for compact storage. The rack measures 7 by 8½ inches. Cost is about $1 from stationers and mail-order firms, including Miles Kimball.

FIG. 9 Keeping your favorite recipes within fingertip reach and ready for use is easy with this Roto-Recipe File (Model RF6-P). Up to 500 recipes may be inserted into the plastic 4 x 5-inch envelopes. Cost is about $6 from stationers, department stores, and mail-order firms. This file is manufactured by the Roto-Photo Company. Or look for an accordion file folder with several dividers; it can hold many different-sized cards or pages.

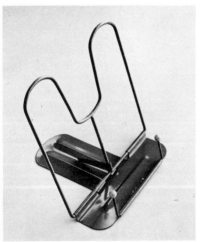
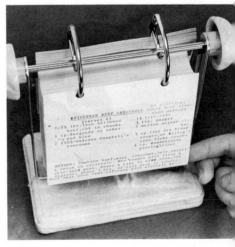

FIG. 8   FIG. 9

FIG. 10 This single recipe card holder can be made at home, or can be purchased at gift shops. It consists of a single dowel, set in a block of wood, topped with a wooden clip clothespin. The bottom of the recipe card slips between the tops of the

FIG. 10

clip. If your cabinets are metal, small magnets will hold a recipe at eye level.

Covering 3 x 5-inch recipe cards with plastic sleeves protects the written matter. A pack of 100 is about $1 at stationery stores or mail-order firms, including Miles Kimball.

Safety in the Kitchen

More accidents occur in the home than anywhere else. When your mobility is limited, it is doubly important to take safety precautions into account. Specific suggestions are given on pages 1 to 36, and on pages 150 to 224. The general ones given below apply to everyone.

WALKING SAFELY

When walking is difficult or slowed by a cane or crutches, be sure to keep your floors skidproof. Don't wax your floors or, if you must, use skidproof wax. Keep a rubber mat on the floor near the sink. When using a walker, cane, or crutches, make sure they are fitted with correct rubber tips.

Wheel, don't carry, whenever possible. (See pages 22 and 23.)

Small spills that are not wiped up could cause you to fall. Clean up both dry and wet spills quickly.

FIG. 1 A long-handled dustpan and brush take care of dry spills, and
may be used while standing or seated, with one or two hands.
This metal dustpan and brush set by G. S. Leiner, or a plastic
set by Easy Day Manufacturing Company, fold up to prevent
your dropping the contents while transferring them to the
wastebasket. Cost of either set is under $5 from department
stores and self-help equipment firms, including J. A. Preston
and Rehab Aids. Similar units are made by Empire Brushes.
Berea Industries manufactures short-handled brooms.

A short-handled sponge mop lets you wipe up wet spots
without bending. Cost is about $1 at variety stores.

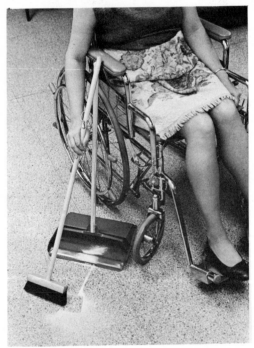

FIG. 1

HANDLING HOT THINGS

Safe, nonflammable potholders are a must especially when your grasp
is weak or you have poor coordination. If sensation is impaired to any
degree, you will need full protection from heat. Asbestos-padded

mitts are thick enough to keep out heat, and the nonflammable covering also provides friction to aid holding. Look for the pebbly-textured asbestos coating made by Welmaid. Cost is about $2 per pair. (See page 184.)

During the spring and summer, elbow-length, asbestos-palmed barbecue mitts are also available from housewares and camping supply stores for about $3 per pair. When reaching is difficult, these longer mitts help prevent your forearms from touching the hot sides of an oven.

FIG. 2 Slide, don't lift, to conserve energy and increase safety when handling pots and pans. This is especially important when your arms are weak, or your hands are affected by arthritis, or you have poor coordination. The best area in your kitchen for you to have a level place for sliding pots is between the sink and the range.

This Rubbermaid Stove 'n Counter mat provides a flat surface next to the range top for resting a hot pan or skillet, while preventing burns or scratches. These aluminum-topped counter mats are available from local houseware stores. Cost is about $1.50 for this model (A8-1321), size 7½ by 19 inches.

The potholder used here has a rubber-waffled surface on one side to help you maintain a more secure grip on a pot handle. It costs about 45¢ at grocery and houseware stores.

FIG. 2

REMEMBERING

Sometimes we have difficulty remembering to turn off ovens and appliances at the right time, or when we are through using them. If this is a problem for you, a visual or audible reminder is suggested.

FIG. 3 A timer will tell you when something is fully cooked or needs looking at. The timer shown here can be operated by a homemaker with weak hands, and set for any time up to an hour. The unit is from Lux Clock Manufacturing Company.

FIG. 4 When you use electrical appliances, a visual reminder telling you to turn off the appliance is often handy. One in the form of a lightbulb or night light, as shown here, can be plugged into an extra socket or may be hooked up between your appliance and the wall outlet. A local electrician can devise a unit for you to use with various appliances. Two units shown under Electricity have such signal lights. (See pages 74 and 75.)

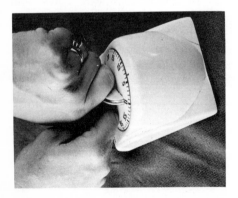

FIG. 3   FIG. 4

FIG. 5 When oil or fat catches on fire, the only way to extinguish the blaze is to smother the flame. If the flame is small, liberal handfuls of salt will smother it. If it's a large oven blaze, turn off the broiler and close the oven door tightly; this will cut off

FIG. 5

the air supply. Never throw water on the flame. The water will only splatter and evaporate, causing more danger to you.

The best answer is to keep a small fire extinguisher near the stove, hanging on a small wall bracket. This Mascot extinguisher (Model PDC 100R), by American La France, weighs one pound, costs about $6, and is Underwriters' Laboratories-approved. To use, simply slip off the small metal guard and press down on the release button. You can use this device with only one hand. If you have severe loss of function in both hands, an elastic cuff holder will help you handle the extinguisher. When buying extinguishers, make sure that they actually can douse oil, fat, electrical, chemical, and other kinds of kitchen fires.

Cooking with Gas

Many homemakers like the quick response of a gas range when they cook. However, if you have difficulty using your hands and do not have an automatic pilot, a few simple techniques may help you deal with the safe lighting of burners and the oven.

FIG. 1 If you have the use of only one hand, or your coordination is poor, you can safely light a non-automatic gas burner by striking a match, laying it across the gas jets, and then turning on

FIG. 1

the gas. With this method, your fingers are kept out of the way and the gas has no chance to accumulate. A small piece of emery or sandpaper taped to the side of the range provides a handy striking surface.

FIG. 2 Lighting the gas broiler and oven requires little or no bending if you use long barbecue or fireplace matches. A 12-inch-long match will reach almost all the way, or can be held in a pair of tongs. Turn on the gas only after you've lit the match. Fireplace matches are sold in department stores and by mail-order firms for about $2 per box. A single match may be used several times.

FIG. 3 When bending is difficult, it's easier to use the broiler if you have long-handled barbecue tools. With a long fork or spatula, you can reach foods in the broiler from a seated position. If lifting is difficult, use lightweight foil broiler pans. Remove the hot meat with a long-handled tool, and leave the foil pan in the broiler until it cools. Then use the tongs or a long spatula to take it out.

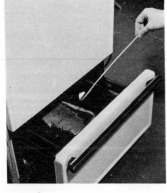

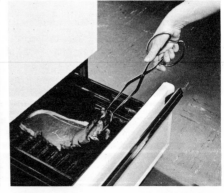

FIG. 2   FIG. 3

FIG. 4 When you must move slowly or are working from a wheelchair at a standard 36-inch-height range, a heat diffuser or flame tamer reduces splatter, helps prevent the bottom of pans from scorching, and serves as a semi-double boiler without raising the pot height. Look for a heat diffuser with a long, non-flammable and non-heat-conducting handle that's easy to move on or off the burner. Cost is about $1.70 from department and culinary specialty stores. Manufacturers include Chicago Metallic Manufacturing Company (Catalog No. 497).

The gas burners shown here are lined with aluminum foil bibs to make clean-up easier. Cost is about 40¢ a set from variety stores. Manufacturers include Chicago Metallic Manufacturing Company.

FIG. 4

FIG. 5 A small top-of-the-stove oven serves as a substitute for your regular oven when heating or baking small amounts of foods. This Everedy Tater Baker (Model 8590) can be used with the trivet to heat casseroles and frozen foods, such as potpies and stews, to brown rolls or biscuits, and to bake meat loaf and potatoes. Without the trivet, it bakes apples and custards and heats baby food. This unit comes with directions for use on gas, kerosene, or electric ranges, or hot plates. In all cases, a low-to-medium flame or dial-setting is recommended. A gauge on the top indicates Warm, Bake, and Hot temperatures. Cost of this stove-top oven is about $7.25 at local houseware and hardware stores.

"Tater Baker" may be used with any ovenproof dish not over 7¼ inches in diameter. A Utility Pan (Model No. 9035), exactly 7¼ inches in diameter and finished in chrome, is available for $1 from your dealer or the Everedy Company.

FIG. 5

Electricity

Today electricity is one of the homemaker's hardest-working servants. If you stop to think how often you rely on this "house-power," you'll realize what an enormous energy-saver it is.

Electricity is such a familiar element that we often take it for granted. During the past twenty years, the number of home appliances requiring electricity has increased from 40 to over 200. To many of us, such items as mixers and stoves have become necessities. However, our household power supply is stretched thinner and thinner with each new energy-saver we plug in. It has been estimated that more than half of all houses in the United States need to be rewired, simply to catch up.

If you depend on electricity to handle many of your mealtime tasks, it might be a good idea to check on your household's electrical capacity. The following signs will tell you that your house is inadequately wired. Watch out if:

1. Lights dim when several appliances are being used.

2. You have trouble with fuses blowing, or circuit breakers tripping off.

3. You require two- and three-way sockets around the house to accommodate lights and appliances.

4. You have to disconnect some appliances before you are able to use others.

If any of these are problems, then obviously there isn't enough electricity running through your wires. You'll find that appliances won't work at peak efficiency, motors will burn out sooner, and lights will dim.

Appliances can be classified as heating and nonheating units. Heating appliances, such as toasters, skillets, or broilers, require a lot of power and should be used one at a time. Nonheating appliances, such as can openers and mixers, require less power and generally can be used simultaneously.

The number of appliances that can be used at the same time depends on the number of amps. or watts each unit requires. To figure out power requirements, simply multiply amps. by volts to get the wattage. For example, if you have an electric frypan listed at 15 amps., 120 volts, it will use up about 1,800 watts. An electric can opener, on the other hand, uses only about 100 watts. Ask your electrician how many watts your circuit can take. If you want to use several heating appliances at once, have the electrician check your wiring system. He may recommend that you add another circuit.

In selecting an electric appliance, make sure it has been approved by Underwriters' Laboratories, a nonprofit testing firm that tests products for manufacturers to provide your assurance of safety.

Three-pronged grounded plugs and outlets are safest, but they're not always available. Whenever there's a choice, select the grounded unit to protect yourself against electric shock. Occasionally you may have to use an extension cord. Make sure that you have a heavy-duty, #16 approved heating cord on all heating appliances.

If your kitchen work area is being remodeled, electrical outlet strips may be built into facings of back-of-the-counter storage or cabinets. The strips can be placed vertically or horizontally, whichever is convenient for you. Leave plugged in and ready appliances you often use that have separate On-Off controls, such as mixers and can openers. Electrical outlet strips are manufactured by General Electric, and are available through electrical contractors and supply stores. Short appliance cords, two feet long, are available from hardware and electrical supply stores. Manufacturers include General Cable Corporation.

FIG. 1 Occasionally an appliance with design features you like may have no On-Off switch. For safety's sake, rectify this by buying a cord with a switch. Take the appliance or cord with you to your electrical supply store, or measure the space between the prongs to determine the correct size. Sometimes, you won't be able to purchase a plug to fit. For example, if the unit has a set-in plug, the cutout will be too small.

The heavy-duty appliance cord shown here has an On-Off switch and a T-handle to make it easy for a person with a weak grasp to pull out the plug. However, the switch requires firm pressure to flick on or off, and may be built up for greater ease. Make sure that the cord is UL-approved and that it is insulated. (A woven fabric cover on the cord indicates that it is insulated.)

FIG. 1

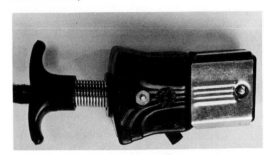

FIG. 2 When an electric appliance is excellent in every other way, except that it lacks an On-Off switch, a line switch can be inserted in the cord to permit you to turn the unit on and off

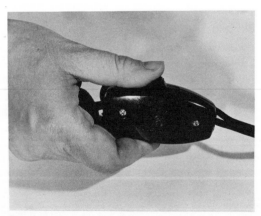

FIG. 2

without pulling out the plug. However, flicking such a switch requires the fairly good use of one hand. Line switches cost about 60¢ apiece at hardware stores. Make sure that they are UL-listed. Manufacturers include General Electric.

FIG. 3 If taking plugs in and out of sockets is difficult or impossible, use this small switch control. It may be inserted directly into the socket, and the switch can be turned on and off with the back of the hand or a thumb. The positive-action switch shown here (15 amps., 125 volts, AC) is especially handy when a unit lacks a built-in On-Off switch. It is manufactured by General Electric and costs about $1.30 at electrical supply stores and from mail-order firms. If vision is impaired, place a small piece of red tape on the side which indicates Off.

NOTE: A switch control is not powerful enough to use with heating appliances such as a broiler or oven.

FIG. 3

FIG. 4 This multiple socket unit is especially helpful when grasp is impaired in both hands, because it is easier to push a regular plug *down* into an outlet rather than into a wall. Hold the plug with the heels of both hands to provide more stability and force. This unit has an On-Off switch for safety, a light to show when it is on, and a 15-amp. fusestat to prevent overloading. Cost is about $5 to $9 at hardware and department stores, or Fedtro, Inc.

FIG. 4

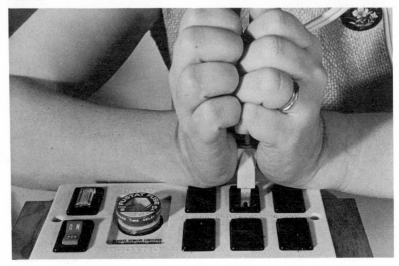

NOTE: Move the unit into the most convenient position while plugging. Then push it out of the way to avoid spilling liquid on it. This could cause a short circuit.

FIG. 5 Special plug-in units can be devised by your local electrician to meet your needs. This unit allows you to leave appliances plugged in when not in use. A signal light tells you when the current is on.

A rocker switch, clearly marked, is operated with light pressure from the heel of the hand.

A tap switch, like the ones used for wall plates, also requires only very light pressure to turn on and off. (This unit was designed by the Electro-Engineering Department, Institute of Rehabilitation Medicine.)

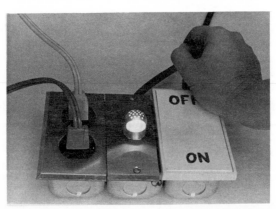

FIG. 5

FIG. 6 This drop-in plug unit was designed to meet the needs of handicapped homemakers and workers by engineers at the Campbell Soup Company. The plug is dropped into the space provided for it, then the cover is lowered and pressed lightly. A red light comes on to tell you that the circuit is connected. Until the cover is lowered, contact is not made; thus, everyone is safer with this unit than with a regular outlet. This unit was tested with severely handicapped individuals, all of whom found it easy to use. For further information, write to Mrs. Judith Klinger, O.T.R., Campbell Soup Fund, Institute of Rehabilitation Medicine, New York University Medical Center, 400 East 34th Street, New York, New York 10016.

FIG. 7 If your hands are weak, or their function is limited by arthritis or incoordination, handling plugs is often difficult. You may circumvent the problem by leaving a unit with an On-Off switch plugged in at all times. When this is not possible, the plug itself may be adapted.

This standard appliance plug is fitted with a wooden dowel and a scalloped top-piece. Push against the wide surface to insert the plug, and hold your fingers around the scalloped piece to pull it out. The plug is fixed to the wood with epoxy glue.

FIG. 8 When grasp is very weak or impaired, a plug with an hourglass neck can be adapted with a loop of cord to help pull the plug out. You can do this only with hourglass-shaped plugs, as the cord will slip with other plugs. Never pull on the cord, as it loosens the wire connections inside the plug itself.

FIG. 6   FIG. 7   FIG. 8

Selecting Small Appliances

Small electrical appliances make meal preparation faster and more fun. Time-consuming tasks, like dicing, whipping, and slicing, which are difficult under any circumstance, can easily be accomplished with the correct use of basic appliances. Place these portable devices where they will be most convenient—on a counter, low table, lapboard, or on the dining-room table.

The types of appliances available to today's homemaker run the gamut from a basic hand-mixer to combination units that grind, crush, mix, or broil and bake. When looking at electrical appliances, consider your own cooking patterns and select the items that are genuinely useful to you.

Some basic portable appliances, like hot plates, broilers, and broiler-ovens, are a great help if you can't manage a large range, and are unable to exchange it for a more suitable one.

The following sections deal with several popular appliances, noting special features to check on when you are purchasing a unit, and ways to adapt controls and other design elements to make them work better for you. The examples given here are representative, not all-inclusive, and should merely be considered as a guide.

Be sure to consult the section on Electricity when considering two or more portable appliances. The discussion on power requirements and aids in handling plugs may be of interest to you. (See pages 70 to 75.)

When you select small appliances, apply the same criteria you used in selecting kitchen equipment. (See page 56.)

Be sure that you can handle the unit easily and that you have no trouble picking it up, moving it about, or, for example, opening or closing doors.

The appliance should have built-in safety features, as well as switches and controls that adjust quickly for you.

The unit should be easy to clean. It should be smoothly designed with accessible surfaces.

It should be versatile and fill more than one need. For example, if you are looking at a coffeemaker, will it make two cups of coffee for breakfast, as well as six for company?

Pre-shopping advice: Before you head for the stores, do some homework. Clip and compare ads from magazines and newspapers. Check reports on recent developments in testing magazines. Talk with your friends about the appliances they use, and find out how they like them. When visiting, ask to try your friends' appliances, and see how comfortable these units are for you. Find out how much room you have for an appliance. Is the place where you intend to set it roomy enough? Of the right height? If space is tight, write down the measurements.

At the store: Be prepared with a list of the features you require in your appliance. Read all hangtags and guarantees. Check to see that instructions are clear. Find out if the appliance needs special care, and what the servicing arrangements are. Check to see whether the appliance is Underwriters' Laboratories listed, and that the UL label does not merely refer to the cord.

Look at the appliance. Pick it up and try out the controls.

Check the construction to make sure there are no rough edges or loose parts. Look at the control markings. Are they easy to read and durable? Finally, select a brand made by a manufacturer with a good reputation that has the features you need in your appliance for maximum assistance in your kitchen.

GUARANTEES AND WARRANTIES

When you buy an appliance, you expect it to be free of defects or problems. Usually this is true, but unfortunately a defective unit may reach the market. This is why manufacturers often stand behind their products with some kind of guarantee or warranty.

The terms guarantee and warranty are used interchangeably. Both vary widely in the services they promise. An appliance can be guaranteed for a ten-day, home-trial period, or for the lifetime of the product. However, there's usually a time limit of one to five years.

Most guarantees and warranties have certain requirements the purchaser must fulfill in order to be eligible. First, you may be asked to send in a registration card within a specified time. If you don't validate the guarantee within this time, your appliance isn't protected.

Secondly, your guarantee or warranty can be voided if you misuse, damage willfully, tamper with, or have your appliance repaired by an unauthorized service dealer. To keep your guarantee in effect, you must go to an authorized dealer. When purchasing an appliance, check the list of authorized dealers. Is there one near you? Are you buying an appliance that can be sent through the mail without undue expense? Check to see who will make good on the guarantee—the manufacturer or the store that sells the item. Check also to see whether the address for the manufacturer is given.

What does the guarantee or warranty cover? Parts only, or parts *and* labor? Does it cover replacement parts? Who pays for the servicing? Is the entire product guaranteed or only specific parts? Are parts readily available, or is this the last of the particular model? Brand-name units are usually easier to repair.

Read all tags and instructions carefully and save them in a convenient place. Mark them with date of purchase. They are your record and guarantee of service. If you misplace the terms and places of contact, it's often hard to trace the responsible party.

CAN OPENERS

A good can opener should cut the lid out completely, leaving a smooth, not sharp, rim. The lid should also raise for easy removal. Often this is done by a magnet. The opener should support the can while it's being cut, so that you don't have to hold it.

If you have difficulty using your hands, other factors are involved. Check the following features in making your selection.

1. Will you be using the can opener with one or two hands? If you work with one hand, then choose a unit that does not require you to hold the can to open it, or select a device that works when you set the can on a sponge while you manipulate the controls. In the latter case, you may be able to adapt your present opener if it has a vertically straight cutting blade.

2. Do the controls move easily? When you have difficulty with both hands, you need controls requiring minimal pressure to operate. An electric can opener with a mechanically linked cutting blade and gear wheel is much easier to use, because the motor activates the cutting blade. Ask for a power-piercing blade. When

manual pressure is required, you may have difficulty making the initial cut. Long levers or extended controls that work with downward pressure are usually the easiest to manage. Occasionally, you may prefer a sliding bar.

If your hands are affected by arthritis, you should select a unit that permits the heel of the hand or the full palm to do the pressing.

3. Can you move the opener if necessary? Not all of us have ample room in our kitchen to keep a can opener in an accessible place. You may wish to slide the unit from the back to the front of the counter when you use it. Occasionally, you may have to lift the unit while operating it. If you have poor coordination, you will need a sturdy unit with a wide or stable base and more weight to prevent tipping.

4. Is the cutting blade easy to see, yet protected so you can't cut yourself? At first, you may want to remove the magnet, until you get to the point where you have developed facility in placing cans under the cutting blade.

5. Is the can opener easy to wipe clean?

6. Finally, try out your selection in the store before you buy it. If testing is not possible, make sure you can return the can opener after trying it out at home. Check both your guarantee and warranty.

FIG. 1 This Universal can opener (Model UC-7), by General Electric, works well for people with limited use of both hands. (This applies to many disabled—quadriplegics, other individ-

FIG. 1

uals with two weak hands, arthritics, and amputees with two
artificial arms.) However, the can must be held up to the
slanted cutting blade. The slide lever requires only light hand
pressure to lock the can in place and activate the motor. This
opener cannot be used with one hand and sponges, as the cutting blade slants too much. It comes with a bottle opener on
the side, an optional knife sharpener on top, and a measuring
table on the back. Cost is about $16.

FIG. 2 This electric Can-O-Matic opener, by Rival Manufacturing
Company, works well for persons with limited strength in the
upper extremities, especially those who are able to hold the
can up to the cutting blade. Light pressure on the long, steel
lever power-pierces the can and cuts open the lid. The unit
shuts off automatically when the can is opened; a magnet
holds the lid.

This opener works for all except the tallest cans. List price
is about $20 to $23. However, it cannot be used for one-
handed function, as the cutting blade slants too much.

FIG. 2

FIG. 3 This Ronson Can-Do electric can opener is designed for use with one hand. The entire opener is lifted over the can, and the cutting blade rests just inside the rim. Light depression of the handle lever activates the motor; the drive wheel turns the can as it cuts.

You can use the Can-Do opener with either your right or your left hand. A magnet holds the lid. This opener comes with a mixer and knife sharpener and costs from $20 to $23, or slightly more, at department stores and self-help firms, including Cleo Living Aids, G. E. Miller, and Rehab Aids. You may also write directly to the Ronson Corporation for the name of the distributor in your area.

FIG. 4 This Farberware can opener (Model 240A) has a power-activated drive-wheel that helps make the initial cut. It's also equipped with a straight cutting blade. Thus, if you are working with one hand, you can set the can on sponges at the correct height, and then with the same hand turn on the controls. Once the can is open, the power automatically stops. Aluminum cans may require slight manual pressure to complete the cutting process. After the can is open, push the button toward the free side.

This can opener works well for people with normal use of one hand or partial use of both hands. Arthritics, however, find that too much finger pressure is required to push the controls. List price is about $14.

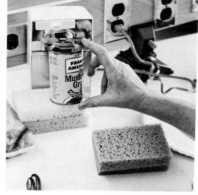

FIG. 3   FIG. 4

FIG. 5 This Westinghouse automatic electric can opener (Model HC 11) has a straight, power-piercing, cutting blade that can be used with one or two hands. Here a partially useful right hand stabilizes the rim of the can under the cutter blade, while the left hand (which operates the slide-bar control) removes the can once the top is released. The power stops automatically once the can is open. List price is about $15.

FIG. 6 This Swing-Away, Vacu-Base manual can opener suctions to any nonporous surface. Thus, it's always within easy reach, even if you're using a wheelchair lapboard. The small lever that attaches or releases the base can be manipulated with the thumb or heel of the hand.

You can adapt this opener for one-handed use by stacking sponges under the can until the lip slips under the cutting blade. Turning the gear-driven handle clockwise opens the can; a counter-clockwise rotation releases it. A magnet holds the lid. Price is about $8 at department stores or from the Swing-Away Manufacturing Company.

FIG. 5

FIG. 6

FIG. 7 This Swing-Away can opener (No. 407M) has a larger key than most portable manual units. If you have moderate grasp in both hands, and need to have a unit you can bring close to you, this can opener may work well. The large key can be turned with the heel of the hand, and because it is gear-driven, will rotate freely. Plastic-coated handles help your grasp. A magnet holds the lid of the can. Unit costs about $3 at houseware and department stores.

FIG. 7

TABLE RANGES

If you're confined to a wheelchair or work at a low surface, and extensive kitchen remodeling isn't possible, then a portable electric hot plate may be an inexpensive solution. It can be used in combination with other appliances. A two-burner hot plate may be placed at a convenient work surface, such as a counter or table; or, if it is to be used only occasionally, at a drop-leaf table.

Look for a unit with the following features:

Low-to-the-counter styling. This eliminates the need to lift pans up and down.

Tubular-type cooking elements. These lift up and thus are easier to clean. Open wire coils are more dangerous.

Large, easy-to-turn control knobs. These should be located at the front of the unit for convenient and safe use.

Infinite heat controls. Controls should range from High to Medium to Low, so that you may quickly adjust cooking temperatures.

A satisfactory two-burner unit will cost about $25 to $30. Unfortunately, less expensive models often do not stand up very well.

FIG. 1 This Nesco, two-burner table range has different controls on each tubular unit. The left control goes from Low to Medium,

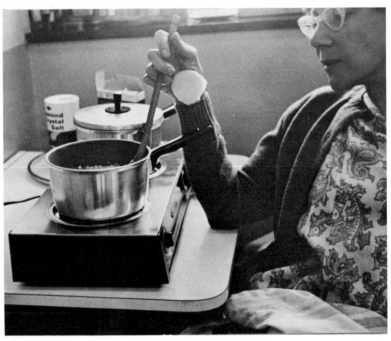

FIG. 1

the right from Low to High. This unit is finished in brushed chrome and black plastic, with built-in sides that make it easy to move or slide. It measures 18 by 10¼ by 4 inches high. Power is 1,650 watts, 120 volts, AC only. This table range is the only unit available with a three-prong grounding plug and a heavy-duty, three-wire cord (Model N125HO). Cost is about $32. Without grounding provision, the model illustrated (N125) is about $30. Similar nongrounded models are available from several manufacturers, including Sears Roebuck (6823), for about $20.

FIG. 2 When lifting is a problem and you're designing a low work area for mealtime preparation, you may wish to incorporate a dropped well for a two-burner range. This will permit you to slide a pan to and from a cooking top, as you would on a larger stove.

The bases on most hot plates will not overheat, but you may wish to line the well with strips cut from a metal-surfaced asbestos mat. These may be tacked along the inside of the well. Another mat may be cut to fit the bottom.

Do not attach the cooking unit to a counter or table, so that you can move the unit to wipe up occasional spills. Make sure the unit you select has front controls and that the well is deep enough. You may also want to leave a few inches of counter space in front of the well to rest cooking tools on.

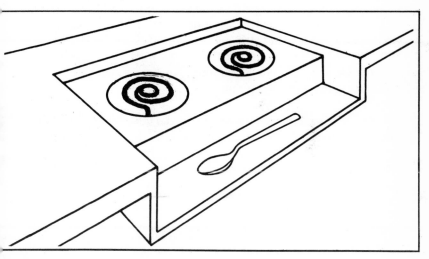

FIG. 2

ELECTRIC SKILLETS

Electric skillets are one of the most versatile of all appliances. Many homemakers find that they rely on these frypans to do most of their cooking. In cases where only minimal kitchen changes are possible, you may find that a skillet allows you to prepare full meals for yourself and your family. Handicapped students living on their own often use electric skillets to prepare breakfast as well as dinner. Casseroles work well in preparing one-dish meals, but aren't as versatile as skillets. However, if you have loss of coordination, you may prefer the deeper-sided casseroles to prevent splattering.

All electric skillets have thermostatically controlled heat ranging from Warm to Hot (150° to 450°). Once the heat-control has been removed, all models are completely immersible. Most electric skillets require 1,200 to 1,600 watts, 120 volts, AC.

Consider the following specific features when purchasing an electric skillet.

Size and weight: Is the unit easy to handle? Square skillets, 11 or 12 inches square, are compact and usually easy to manage. Weights vary from model to model. Select a unit that is thick enough to provide good, even cooking. It's not always necessary to lift the unit. You can cook in one place and slide it out of the way when you're finished. Or you can cook at the table, or have someone else bring the skillet to the table for serving.

Material: Aluminum and stainless steel skillets are the easiest to manage. Porcelain or polymide finishes on the outside of skillets come in a range of brilliant colors for attractive, at-the-table serving. Several brands also have nonstick linings. A fired-on, Teflon II finish is recommended. Units with softer coatings mar quickly and are hard to clean.

Handle design: The handle should be, and usually is, of non-heat-conducting material. The placement of handles is important in enabling you to maneuver the skillet safely and easily. A single handle may be preferred if you are using only one hand. However, if you have loss of power in both upper extremities, you should look for a unit with double handles that are large enough to grasp or hook-grasp easily. The handles should have an inner baffle to prevent your fingers from coming in contact with the hot metal when lifting.

Control: The temperature control should be located so that you can insert it and turn it easily. Controls placed under a handle are hard to manage. The knob itself should be large enough to grasp and have ridged edges. A baffle in back of the control prevents your accidentally touching the hot metal and burning your fingers. When fingers are very weak, you may need to adapt the control. The temperature reading should be large enough to see easily. A signal light should tell you when the proper temperature has been reached.

Cover: The knob on the cover should be high enough and located so that you can pick it up without touching the metal with your fingers or forearm. You may have to adapt the knob. The cover should be vented so that you can brown foods without their becoming soggy. Some models have a tilt cover that shields the countertop from splatter while you baste or turn food. High-domed covers permit you to use the skillet for baking or cooking large roasts. Optional broiler lids are available with some brands. A broiler device snaps in and out of the cover. When in use, the heat control is connected to the device in the lid.

Other features: A bake or roast rack increases versatility. Legs set far enough out from the edge help in lifting while draining grease and serving foods.

Before using your skillet, read the instruction book carefully. Some skillets must be seasoned with salad oil or unsalted shortening, and then washed before you begin to cook. Also check the amount of time that yours takes to preheat. Most skillets come with a signal light that goes off when the set temperature is reached.

Many recipes call for you to simmer ingredients for extended periods. Since the boiling point of water is affected by differences in altitude and other conditions, test to find the simmering temperature for your skillet in this way. First, pour 4 cups of water into the skillet. Cover, leaving the steam vents open. Plug the temperature control into the skillet, then plug the cord into the outlet. Set the control at 250°. The water will soon begin to boil. After 10 minutes, slowly turn the temperature control down just until the light goes off. This is your simmering temperature. Mark it on the control, or write it down so you remember it.

To insert a skillet control when using one hand or when both hands are weak, you may either set the skillet on a rubber mat so that it does not slide, or push the skillet all the way to the back of the counter so that it is stabilized against the wall. Rubbermaid makes a waffled protector mat (No. 1305) that is 15½ by 17 inches, and costs about $1.30 at houseware stores. (See page 173)

Always turn your skillet temperature control completely off and remove the plug from the wall socket before removing the control from the skillet itself.

You will find that you can use your skillet for a number of different cooking processes, including pan broiling, roasting meat, baking casseroles, heating frozen prepared meals or brown-and-serve rolls, and simmer-steaming single servings of baby food or special foods. A small rack, which can be placed in the skillet for baking and heating foods, is available from mail-order firms for about $1. To heat frozen prepared dinners, add about ½ cup of water to the skillet.

FIG. 1 This 12-inch-diameter electric skillet (Model 2272, 2274, or 2275), by Dominion, is lined with Teflon II and comes with a frying basket, which can be used for draining vegetables and other foods, or for cooking several immersible bags at one time.

The removable heat control turns easily, but does not have rough ridges. It may be adapted with a dowel if necessary. The immersible skillet is finished with baked-on enamel in several colors. Price is about $24 to $32 at department and appliance stores.

FIG. 1

FIG. 2A This electric skillet-broiler by Westinghouse is a versatile appliance. The control has a slanted surface with a slight baffle to keep your hand away from the hot pan. The open handles are designed with a baffle next to the pan so that you can use a hook grasp to pick up the skillet or maneuver it. The cover handle at the side is helpful if you have weak shoulders and find it difficult to reach over and grasp the knob. It does, however, require fairly good grasp or a hook type of grasp.

FIG. 2A

FIG. 2B

FIG. 2B Two holes in the cover create a safety problem, because they allow steam to escape when the broiler coil is removed for normal use of the skillet. To overcome this, and to prevent burning your forearm, insert a small block of wood into the space, to cover the holes. This block of wood was designed with a cutout hole for easier removal; it also serves as a balancing aid when you're putting on the cover or removing it with two weak hands.

FIG. 3 The cover knob on this electric skillet was replaced with an open wooden handle to permit someone with loss of grasp to lift the cover more safely and easily.

Most skillet cover knobs are attached with a single screw which removes easily. A new handle may be fashioned at home or purchased from a hardware store. Make sure that the material is heat-resistant.

FIG. 4 When pinch is weak or lacking in both hands, turning knobs is difficult. Two hands provide adequate power to easily rotate the control on this skillet. The baffle in back of the control knob protects the hand from touching the hot metal.

FIG. 3

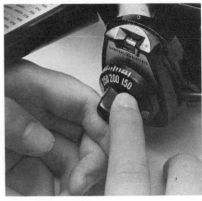

FIG. 4

This skillet by General Electric (Model C126T) has a single long handle and is lined with Teflon. List price is about $27. Sears Roebuck also makes a frypan with a single handle (34A 6525). Cost is about $13.

FIG. 5 When the temperature control on an electric skillet, casserole, or similar appliance is difficult and dangerous to turn because your hands are weak, uncoordinated, or affected by arthritis, you may adapt it. This metal-spoked handle is designed so that an individual hits the spokes with the back of the hand to adjust the temperature. It is attached to the center of a stand-

FIG. 5

ard skillet control, in this case a Presto Control Master, with four metal screws. A similar unit could be constructed by a local metalworker or adapted with wooden dowels and metal screws.

FIG. 6 When you cannot grasp the knob of a skillet cover, one solution is to hook it with the tines of a large fork, and hoist it, using both hands to balance the cover. This skillet by Sunbeam (Model VRLB) has double handles set out from the pan so they are easy to grasp, and a tilt handle on the cover. List price is about $23.

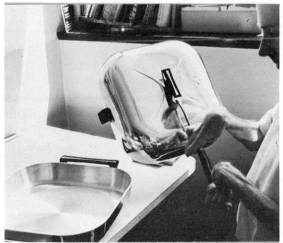

FIG. 6

FIG. 7 This Electric Country Kettle, by West Bend, may be used for stewing, roasting, frying, and other forms of cooking. Temperature may be adjusted from Warm to 400°. Although the thick aluminum sides become hot while in use, the flat handles and cover knob stay cool. The handles extend far enough for a person with weak upper extremities or arthritis to manipulate the kettle without difficulty. The control dial is ridged on the outer rim to insure a more secure grip. Persons with loss of hand function, however, may wish to add a dowel extension for easier rotation. Country Kettle comes in Avocado or Harvest Gold for attractive serving at the table, and lists for about $28 at department and appliance stores.

FIG. 7

BROILERS, OVENS, AND BROILER-OVENS

A good, portable broiler-oven can often substitute for a regular oven when major kitchen remodeling is not possible. This portable unit can be placed on a countertop at the most convenient level for you. It's a good idea to provide a resting area for pans of food in front of the unit, especially if your upper extremities are so weak that carrying is difficult or unsafe.

Unfortunately, many broilers, ovens, and broiler-ovens on the market do not have adequate safety features. Many lack an On-Off switch. However, all the units given here (with two exceptions) have On-Off controls, doors that operate safely with practice, and adequate temperature controls. Some of these units do have unstable pull-out shelves and controls that are difficult to turn, but solutions for both these problems are given.

Portable electric ovens and broilers vary a great deal in their ability to reach and maintain specific temperatures. It's wise to test your unit with an oven thermometer, and to vary the rack height the first few times you bake, until you have determined the best arrangement.

Consider what you want to use the appliance for. Are you going to use it as a daily substitute for your oven—or mainly for heating and broiling? The extra cost of a good portable oven is well worth the expense if you plan to use this unit for baking.

Three basic types of units are available: the enclosed broiler, oven, or broiler-oven; the open broiler; and the round, closed broiler.

ENCLOSED BROILER-OVENS

Be sure to look for the following features in an enclosed broiler, oven, or broiler-oven.

Broil and bake elements: These are located at the top and bottom of your unit. Tubular elements are more durable than wire or coil-type. For best distribution of heat, look for an element that does not merely go around the top in a rectangle, but is formed to cross over the center of the area. Removable elements make it easier to clean the interior.

Interior: Check the size to make sure that it will fit your baking pans. This type of unit splatters while broiling. The lining should be smooth and accessible so that it may be easily cleaned.

Racks and rack supports: Racks and pans should be heavy enough so that they do not warp when heated; but also lightweight enough for you to lift. Broiling pans should be deep enough to hold a substantial amount of fat without spilling when you remove the pan from the oven. Slotted racks are better than open wire racks, as they reduce the chances of grease flaring up. Several units come with supports for the racks but many of these are not dependable.

To accommodate different kinds of foods, several rack positions should be offered. Side wall supports should hold the rack securely when pulled out about two thirds of the way. Many do not and have to be adapted. Check to see that you can pull out the tray without the oven sliding on the counter.

Controls: On combination broiler-ovens, there should be a thermostatic control from about 250° to 450°. Are the control knobs large enough for you to turn? You should be able to operate them without touching the metal. Several units have push buttons to set the oven on Bake, Broil, and Off. Others have switches. Make sure that you can switch from Bake to Broil without having to unplug and plug the switch in a different socket. This is dangerous, as the oven may be very hot; often this type does not have an On-Off switch.

Several units have automatic timers that turn the unit off after a preset time has elapsed, which is an excellent idea, especially if you are forgetful. Also look for a signal light that tells you when the correct temperature is reached.

Door: Can you open and close the door easily? Is the handle large enough for you to hold without touching the metal; is it of non-heat-conducting material? Ask the salesman. Because a handle is not metal does not mean that it will not get too hot to handle. Always use a potholder, in any case.

Does the door stay on its hinges when you open and close it quickly? Some doors take skillful maneuvering to open and close easily, and a few tend to stick when heated.

Insulation: Check to see what type of insulation the oven walls have, especially if you plan to use the unit for baking. Snug-fitting doors are also important in helping to keep the temperature at an even level.

Power requirements: Make sure that you have wiring equal to the demands the broiler-oven will place on it. All of these units are 120 volts, AC only, but they have a range of 1,320 to 1,650 watts.

FIG. 1 This General Electric broiler-oven (R-30) works well for both baking and broiling as a substitute for a standard range. The interior will hold two 8-inch layer cake pans, two square pans, or two frozen prepared dinners. The sides and base slide out for cleaning. The stainless steel exterior is smooth and easy to keep clean. The compact design allows you to set it at the back of a standard-depth counter and still have space to work in front of it. The tubular broiling element gives even surface-heat distribution. The broiler tray has a slotted surface.

Push buttons control the Broil, Bake, and Rotisserie switches. The temperature control is ridged along the outer surface and, although small, will turn easily. A timer, com-

FIG. 1

bined with the On-Off switch, is harder to turn, and here has been adapted with a dowel. If you are using the rotisserie, the meat turns automatically.

Shelf supports in this model are excellent; the rack is supported on both the top and bottom so that it cannot fall when you pull it out. If you wish, you can purchase a second shelf for this oven from General Electric Service Center stores for about $3.60.

There is a metal rod handle far enough away from the door for you to grasp it easily with a potholder. Since the rod lies almost flush with the counter, you may wish to leave a potholder under it to make it easier to open the door. The door has to be lifted slightly up and out to open it. Power is 1,500 watts, 120 volts, AC only. List price is about $90. Montgomery Ward carries a similar unit.

FIG. 2 This Golden Chef broiler-oven rotisserie (Model 99) by Black Angus, Inc., has push-button controls, including one for a timed outlet. The outlet can only be used when the oven is off, but then can be coupled with another electric appliance, like a skillet, to permit a specific period of cooking. The heat control is not measured in degrees, but is graded according to Off, Warm, Low Bake, Moderate, High Bake, Rotisserie, and Broil. The On and Off cycling of the element is automatically controlled. The timer must be turned on to operate the unit, and may be adapted with a dowel. A pilot light indicates when the timer is on.

This unit comes with an interchangeable element, but you should buy a second element if you bake or broil frequently. Shelf supports on the upper level are double, but bottom sup-

FIG. 2

ports need additional brackets. Golden Chef comes with an aluminum broil pan, a combination bake-and-broil drip pan, a rack, spit, and skewers. Shelves are 16½ inches wide and 12 inches deep, and thus hold two 8-inch layer cake pans or two frozen prepared dinners. Power is 1,600 watts, 120 volts, AC. Cost is about $50.

The Black Angus Malibu Oven, on page 26, is similar but also has a lift-up grill top for heating foods. Cost is about $70.

FIG. 3 This 19" broiler-oven by Ronson has push-button controls for Bake, Broil, and Off; a very easy-to-turn temperature dial, and a signal light that indicates when the oven has reached the desired temperature. Temperature range is from 100° to 500°. An outlet on the front permits you to use other appliances when the push button is in the Off position. Tubular elements are in the top and bottom.

Two levers on the right-hand side adjust the height of the single shelf. The shelf itself, however, needs to have brackets added so that it will not tip. The interior (15 inches wide, 11 inches deep, and 7 inches high) will hold two frozen prepared dinners, but will not hold two 8-inch layer cake pans. The door has a good handle, opens by lifting slightly up and out, and can be removed for cleaning. Cost is about $40 at appliance and department stores.

FIG. 3

FIG. 4 This broiler-oven (2540), by Toastmaster, has thermostatically controlled broiling and baking tubular elements. The temperature range is from 200° to 500°. The broiler may be adjusted to Low, Medium, or High. The controls are located on the top; the temperature dial turns easily. A temperature guide is listed on the control panel.

The unit is compact. A single shelf with top and bottom shelf supports can be slid out without tipping. The broiling tray has a slotted design. The interior measures 14½ inches wide by 11 inches deep and will take two frozen prepared dinners. The door must be lifted to open and removes for cleaning. Sides stay cool so the oven can easily be moved. Power is 1,250 watts, 120 volts, AC only. List price is about $36.

FIG. 4

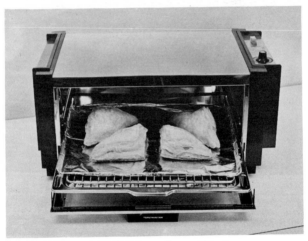

FIG. 5 This Presto oven (Model PO22), 13½ inches wide by 13 inches deep, will hold a full-sized meal on two shelves. The door lifts up out of the way for full access to the oven shelves, but requires fairly good arm-reach to open and close it.

The control is conveniently located on the front. If limited grasp makes turning difficult, a dowel handle can be added. When the control is removed, the entire oven can be immersed for cleaning. The oven keeps a constant temperature and bakes evenly. A reflector plate completely covers the coils for safety. An easy-to-follow temperature guide is located on the front of the door. List price is about $29 at houseware or department stores, or Presto National Industries. Power is 120 volts, 1,500 watts, AC.

NOTE: This unit does not broil.

FIG. 5

FIG. 6 This Black Angus Petite, broiler-toaster-warmer (03303) does what it's supposed to do. That is, it broils and heats food satisfactorily, but it does not hold even temperatures for baking. Side controls click easily into place. The door can be removed for cleaning. Brackets should be added to the shelf to keep it from tipping. Cost is about $25 at department and appliance stores.

It's safer to avoid using the removable handle that comes with many broiler-ovens, because this handle will not always hold the tray securely. If you have poor coordination or bad vision, you may not be able to fit the brackets on the tray correctly. If you have arthritis or weakness in your hands, you'll find that the weight of the tray feels greater at the far end of the handle.

To handle hot pans and trays in the oven, it's best to slide the rack out until you can easily reach the pan itself. The unit may be adapted with brackets, if necessary. The small broiler

FIG. 6

100

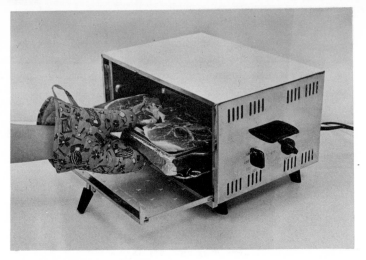

pan shown here is made by Ekco, and measures 7 by 10 inches. It fits almost any broiler-oven, is lightweight, and can be used as a broiler pan with the drip rack, or without it as a regular pan. Cost is about $1 at houseware stores.

FIG. 7 Small, stainless steel brackets screwed to the sides of a broiler-oven just above the rack will keep the oven shelf from tipping when it's pulled out. If stainless steel is not easily available at a local metal shop, buy a stainless steel kitchen spatula (or similar flat tool) and cut small pieces out of the flat section. Two brackets on the front of each shelf will provide adequate stability.

FIG. 8 If a control knob is too small to grasp or is difficult to turn, it can easily be adapted with a small dowel stick attached to the knob with a screw.

FIG. 7

FIG. 8

OPEN BROILERS

Open broilers cook food from below. The food is placed on a rack over a tubular broiling element. Drippings fall into a stainless steel or aluminum drip pan kept cool by construction or by a small amount of water. This type of broiler does not splatter or smoke, as the drippings do not hit a hot surface. Most of these units do not have an On-Off switch but may be adapted with a cord switch or universal plug with an On-Off switch. (See page 72.) Some units come with rotisserie attachments as optional equipment.

Individuals with weak upper extremities and loss of hand function find this type of open grill easy to use, because it eliminates the handling of doors, pans, and racks. Drippings fall into a tray below, which may be lined with foil for easy clean-up.

Features to consider in selecting this unit include the following:

Rack design: A two or more position rack accommodates different kinds of foods.

Ease of disassembling: A removable heating unit and easily disassembled components make cleaning much simpler.

FIG. 9 This stainless steel electric broiler, by Farberware, incorporates a cooling zone in its design to keep it free from smoke and splatter. However, it does not have an On-Off switch, so the appliance cord must be adapted with a cord switch or fitted with an appliance cord with a built-in, On-Off control. (See pages 72 and 73.) Price of the Farberware Open-Hearth broiler with a 10- by 15-inch broiling surface (No. 450-A) is about $30; with an 8½- by 12-inch surface (No. 440), $20. These broilers also come with motorized rotisserie attachments (No. 455-A) for about $45.

Similar units, with rotisseries, are made by Dominion, Toastmaster, and Mirro Aluminum.

FIG. 9

ROUND, CLOSED BROILERS

A small, electric closed broiler is very simple in design. The coil-type broiling element is contained in the high, vented cover. When it's being used, the food is put on a slotted rack with a drip pan, then the cover is placed over the base.

FIG. 10 This electric aluminum broiler unit (Model 0475) by Mirro Aluminum, has a hinged lid which opens to rest on a single heat-resistant handle. This unit is not recommended for you if you have marked incoordination, as the hinge is not attached to the base. The 9½-inch-diameter broiler surface will hold a medium-sized steak, several chicken pieces, chops, or hamburgers. A sponge cloth or rubber mat under the broiler prevents sliding. The bottom is immersible or may be lined with foil so that clean-up involves only a small drip rack.

This model has no On-Off control, but an appliance cord with an On-Off switch to fit the prongs can be purchased from a hardware store. (See page 72.) Power is 490 watts, 120 volts, AC and DC. List price is about $10 at houseware and department stores.

FIG. 10

MIXERS

Mixers come in two basic models: a lightweight, portable hand model, and a heavier stand or counter model. Your choice will probably depend on two factors: one, the amount of mixing you use the unit for; and two, the extent of your weakness or limited functioning of upper extremities. If you bake only occasionally and want to save time and trouble when mixing up batters and mixtures, like mashed potatoes, for instance, then a portable mixer will do. If you wish to use a portable mixer, however, you should have good grasp in one hand, or at least be able to hold the unit in two hands. Many homemakers in wheelchairs find the hand mixer helpful as they are able to put the mixing bowl on a lapboard or in their lap to work.

However, if you do a lot of baking, you may prefer a counter model. Since the heavier unit eliminates holding, you'll probably find it more satisfactory if you have poor coordination or weak upper extremities. The mixer does its own work while you add the ingredients.

PORTABLE HAND MIXERS

Look for the following features when buying a hand mixer.

Weight and handle design: Look for a unit with a handle that is comfortable for you. If your grasp is weak, you may prefer an enclosed handle that won't slip away from you. Very lightweight models often have less power, so a compromise has to be made between weight and power. Try holding the unit in your hand for several minutes to see how it balances.

Heel rest: Make sure that you can set the beaters down on the heel rest easily and that the heel rest is stable. Check to see that the beaters are high enough to extend over the mixing bowl, thus allowing for dripping and scraping and avoiding extra clean-up.

Controls: Make sure you can turn the controls on and off without any difficulty. Check to see that the beater ejectors do not require too much force for you to manage. If you have arthritis in your hands, select a model which will allow you to manipulate controls with the side of one hand, and thus avoid putting too much pressure on the end of your thumb.

Beaters: Beaters that don't have a center shaft are easier to clean. One manufacturer provides two sets of beaters, the extra one coated with nylon to use with Teflon-coated utensils.

Further hints: To insert beaters when your grasp is weak, hold the mixer upside down on your lap, or another surface; then press down on the beaters with the palm of your hand.

Place a damp sponge under a lightweight bowl to keep it from sliding while you're mixing.

Thin rubber spatulas are very useful in helping you to clean beaters. These spatulas, manufactured by Rubbermaid and others, easily slip in between the blades; they're available at local variety stores. Be sure your mixer is turned off before putting a spatula near the blade of the beater.

Spin excess batter off beaters by setting your mixer at its lowest speed (keep the beaters down in the bowl).

Some hand mixers come with such accessories as a stand and bowls, drink-mixer attachments, and a knife sharpener. Although all of these are certainly handy, they're extras. The most important thing to check on is the comfort of the mixer in your hands.

FIG. 1 This Oster Imperial hand mixer (356), with an enclosed handle, is very lightweight and has a raised top control that's easy to maneuver when your hands are weak or lack coordination. The heel rest is stable. The beaters are released by pressing lightly with the palm of the hand on the front plate of the mixer while it's standing on the heel rest. Power is 100 watts, 120 volts, AC. List price is about $12.

A similar unit, the Vista mixer, is made by Sunbeam and lists for $15.

FIG. 2 This Braun portable mixer (M-140) weighs only 2½ pounds yet is powerful enough to mix bread dough. The closed handle makes it easier to support when your grasp is weak. The three-speed control button, located on the top, can be operated by sliding it with the side of the hand. This unit also has an "instant switch" for slow mixing. The ejector button, just in front of the speed control, depresses easily. The beaters have no center shafts and are of heavy wire, so they will clean easily. The heel rest is wide and flat, thus providing good stability. This mixer comes with beaters, a dough hook, and a wall mounting rack for about $20 from appliance and department stores, or write Braun Electric America, Inc.

FIG. 1

FIG. 2

FIG. 3 If you find holding a hand mixer tiring, try different ways to rest it while beating. You may lightly balance the beater on the side of a mixing bowl. Or you may place a mixing bowl in the corner of a dish drainer and rest the motor unit on the edge of the drainer. In this position, the bowl cannot tip. When used with a stainless steel or other thin plastic or metal bowl, the dish drainer is just the right height to accommodate a hand mixer. The mixer shown here is by General Electric and costs about $13.

FIG. 3

STANDARD COUNTER MIXERS

When buying a standard mixer, check several of the same features listed for hand mixers, such as beater design, and the ease with which the controls and beater ejector can be manipulated, and handle weight and design. Other factors might include the following:

Design and weight: Is the unit compact enough to be stored on the counter where it's ready for use? Can you slide it out of the way when it's not in use? Most stand mixers have motor and beater units that detach from the stand for use as a hand mixer. These, however, are usually much heavier than a portable hand mixer.

Bowls: Stainless steel bowls are much easier to handle than glass or ceramic ones, and are available with several models. Be sure to ask for them, since they are optional equipment, and are much more expensive when bought separately.

Speed control: There are usually 9 to 12 speeds on a stand mixer. Look for an easy-to-read guide that tells you what speed is best for specific mixtures.

Motor and hinge: Make sure you can tilt the motor-beater handle back to raise the beaters from the bowl while adding ingredients or scraping the beaters.

Optional accessories include a citrus-fruit juicer, food grinder, vegetable slicer, coffee bean grinder, can opener, knife sharpener, and dough-hook attachment (on the most powerful units). Since the cost varies with the number of accessories you purchase, you must decide on the value of the additions in relation to your own cooking patterns.

FIG. 4 The control on this countertop Mixmaster (Model 12W), by Sunbeam, may be operated with one good hand, or with the heels of both hands when upper extremities are weak. List price is about $56 with stainless steel bowls. To release the beaters, push or hit the large handle down to the side.

FIG. 4

FIG. 5 The controls on this counter model mixer extend far enough out for use under almost any circumstance. Here an amputee manipulates the speed control with her prosthetic device. The lettering is easy to read and follow.

FIG. 6 This Hamilton Beach mixer (Model 021) is compact in size, comes with stainless steel bowls, has a ten-speed control, and lists for about $60. You have to have moderate use of one hand to start the speed control. However, the bowl control knob moves very easily, reducing the need for scraping. Kitchen Aid by Hobart also makes a counter mixer with stainless steel bowls.

FIG. 7 A pop-up mixer shelf for a stand mixer may be installed in a base cabinet. Springs counterbalance the weight of the mixer and the shelf, making it easy to lift up into place. First determine your best working height and then install the unit at this level. Hardware for pop-up shelves is carried by kitchen cabinet manufacturers, including Long-Bell, a division of International Paper Company, and hardware suppliers.

FIG. 5

FIG. 6

FIG. 7

ELECTRIC BLENDERS

An electric blender can accomplish in only a few seconds what ordinarily would take a half hour or more to do. The high-speed motor and rotating blades can blend, mix, chop, grate, puree, liquefy, and shred many types of foods.

If you have marked loss of function in your hands, including weakness, lack of coordination, and arthritis, you'll find a blender helpful, especially if you use a lot of fresh foods. However, in buying a blender, take care to insure that your blender is actually a helpmate. Too-heavy containers, or controls that are difficult to manipulate, for example, could easily turn this device into a hindrance.

When selecting a blender, check on the following.

Base height: The lower the base, the easier it is to add ingredients through the top of the container and to lift the unit on and off the base. The total height from the base to the top of the container usually ranges between 10 to 20 inches. Some bases, however, are only 3½ inches high. A few bases come with lift handles to enable you to move the entire unit from place to place.

Container: Blender containers of high-impact, heat-resistant plastic are much lighter to lift than glass. If you have the use of only one hand, or loss of function in both hands, a handle on the side of the container is helpful. You can hook-grasp the handle and balance the unit with your other hand. Most blender containers hold between 32 to 56 ounces. Measuring marks on the side help when you're adding ingredients and tell you the container's capacity.

Make sure you can lift off the cover to add ingredients. The removable center is usually a 1- or 2-ounce measure.

Take the container's base assembly apart. You'll have to remove it to scrape out food collected at the bottom of the blender. Most base assemblies unscrew. Tightening or loosening is easier if you put the base assembly in the base-holder and turn against the sprockets. A few units have clips to remove base assemblies.

Some container bases are threaded to fit a standard Mason jar. This means that you can use the same container to blend and store food. Other blenders come with ½-pint jars in which you can blend and store small amounts like salad dressing or sauces.

Controls: Most blenders have push button or sliding controls which are easy to manage even when you have marked limitation in the use of your hands. A few units have dials which require moderate grasp in one hand to turn.

Many blenders have a wide variety of speed settings. If you are experienced in using this appliance, you probably can get by with 2 speeds: High and Low. The most you will probably require is 4 or 5 speeds. However, some units have controls that maintain the power at any speed, regardless of the density of the mixture.

Timers are useful if you move slowly. They can be preset to turn off the motor at the suggested time.

Use-and-care and recipe book: Every blender comes with a book of instructions and suggestions telling you how many things your unit can do, which is extremely helpful, especially if you haven't used a blender before. Many cookbooks of blender recipes are also available.

FIG. 1 This Cyclotrol Eight, Imperial Liquifier-Blender (Model 548), by John Oster Manufacturing Company, has a single-handled plastic container with graduated measuring marks. Eight push buttons control the speed. The three buttons on the left, marked Grate, Chop, and Grind, are "cycle operation" buttons. As long as one of these three is held down, the motor operates. As soon as the button is released, the motor shuts off. The container base assembly removes for cleaning. The cover has a removable center for adding ingredients. List price is about $30. Oster Mini-Blend ½-pint containers are available for use with this blender. General Electric also makes a blender (Model BL-1) with a single-handled plastic container, and easy-to-operate sliding controls. List price is about $25.

FIG. 1

FIG. 2 This Hamilton Beach Cookbook blender (256) has a low
silhouette (base height is 3½ inches), making it easy to lift the
plastic container on and off. A built-in spatula, operated from
the top, keeps foods flowing and blending. The container
holds 44 ounces. The whole top is removed to add ingredients.
The 7-speed, solid-state control is operated with a single
lever which can be slid with the side of the hand. Power is 900
watts, 120 volts, AC. It comes with a five-year guarantee and
lists for about $55.

FIG. 2

FIG. 3 This Rival Magic Touch blender (Model 930) has dual, solid-
state controls, which allow you to set both speed and time,
before you turn on the motor. However, you must have ade-

FIG. 3

quate pinch to turn the dials. The heat-resistant, Tyril, 44-ounce container has a single handle, pouring lip, and graduated markings. The removable blade assembly fits canning jars. The vinyl lid has a 2-ounce measuring cup. List cost is about $60.

ELECTRIC KNIVES

The design and type of motor may vary on electric knives, but basically they all operate in the same way. Twin blades are hooked together and inserted into a motorized handle. The handle may be rechargeable and cordless, permitting you to use it anywhere you wish. Or it may be a cord model, in which case the handle is usually smaller. With both models, fingertip controls start the blades sliding back and forth against each other. Releasing the pressure stops the blades.

If you are preparing food for a large family, you may wish to consider an electric knife. It is especially helpful for slicing meat. You should have good grasp in one hand or partial use of both hands, and you should not have any problems with perception if you are planning to use an electric knife. Some women with arthritis in their hands find that a lightweight electric knife eliminates a lot of the stress involved in hand cutting.

Features to check when buying an electric knife include the following:

Weight and balance: Pick up the knife and hold it as though you were cutting. Maintain this position for several minutes and see how the weight feels. Try several brands to get an idea of the differences in balance. When cutting, you can stop to rest and may also put your elbows on the arms of a chair to provide additional support.

Length and handle design: Several models come with smaller grip-sized handles, which may be good if you have normal grasp in one hand. Other styles have open handles; some of these have been used successfully by homemakers with almost complete loss of grasp in both hands. Slipping one hand under the handle supports the knife; the other hand applies pressure to the control to activate the motion of the blades. Also check the length of the handle. Make sure that it is not unwieldy for you.

Controls: You should be able to handle controls quickly and easily, including the safety lock which turns the knife off so that it cannot be started accidentally, as well as the button which starts the blades. Some knives have a dual control button; you have to depress two levers simultaneously to activate the blades.

Also check the blade-release mechanism. It should be located so that you can release the blades without accidentally hitting the switch control at the same time. When releasing the blades, hold the knife slanting down, push the release button, and shake the blades until they slip out part way. Keep your fingers out of the way. With cord models, make sure you disconnect the plug before taking out the blades.

Some knives come with a dual set of blades, one long and one short, for more convenient carving. Another model has switch-blades so that you can cut horizontally or vertically without changing the position of the handle.

An electric knife can be used for many jobs. It can carve all kinds of meats; slice vegetables and fruits; shred salad ingredients; cut cheese, cakes, sandwiches, and ice cream. It should not be used to cut through frozen foods, or through bones, as this dulls the blades and shortens their span of usefulness. When slicing raw meat, place the meat in the freezer for about 20 minutes until it is partially frozen. Then the meat will slice more easily.

Always handle the blades on the smooth side, keeping your fingers away from the cutting edge. The plastic sheath on the blades hooks them together until they are inserted, and protects your hands.

The care of an electric knife is not complicated. The blades should be washed well and dried after each use. The handle may be wiped clean with a sponge. Plastic grease-guards prevent meat juices or fat from getting inside the handle. All cutting should be done on a wooden board, or a specially designed plastic board, to protect the blade edges. The textured surface of a wood board holds the meat stable, even when you're cutting with one hand. The board shown on page 22 is lightweight, attractive, and small enough to handle easily. Cost is about $6 from department stores and mail-order firms, including Maison Michel.

FIG. 1 This Hamilton Beach, cordless, electric carving knife (285) has a hole in the handle. Persons with loss of grasp, including quadriplegics, can operate it by supporting it with one hand under the handle and pressing lightly with the other hand on the top control to activate the blades. An important safety feature here is the dual control; the double pressure points mean that the blades cannot begin to cut if the knife is accidentally dropped. You must lightly depress the lever under the handle at the same time you press down on the top button. If you have loss of grasp, you simply place your hand under the front of the handle, thus depressing the lever.

Some models of this knife come with a blade that pivots from vertical to horizontal for easier carving without your having to shift your grip. To recharge, the unit is placed in a storage tray which is kept plugged in. Hamilton Beach knives come with a 5-year written guarantee, and list for about $18 to $24.

Sunbeam makes a cord model (VEK 500) with an open-grip handle. It lists for about $18.

FIG. 1

FIG. 2 This General Electric cord model (EK-9) has a small, contoured plastic handle for easier grip when there is normal use of one hand. A pin-type safety lock prevents the blades from

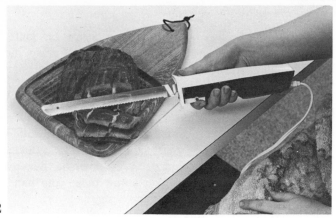

FIG. 2

accidentally starting. The switch bar, located under the handle, is spring-loaded and requires light pressure to maintain blade action. When the blade-release mechanism (located on either side of the handle) is depressed, the blades can be shaken out with one hand. List price is about $20.

TOASTERS

Most toasters are slot-type units that hold the bread slices in an upright position. For those who prefer a variety of toasted breads and rolls, an oven-type unit that holds the bread on a horizontal rack may be preferred.

Slot-type toasters come in 2- or 4-slice models, but will toast only one slice, if desired. They vary widely in price and quality, so check the quality of construction, safety features, and controls carefully before purchasing. The following checkpoints may help.

Timing mechanism: The thermostat should be quick to heat up and to cool off. It should automatically compensate for any voltage fluctuations in your home. Ask the salesperson if the toaster will toast consecutive slices to the same degree of brownness.

Controls: Are the lever that presses the toast down and the toast-color control dial located where you can reach and turn them conveniently? Can you operate them without touching the hot metal? Ask if the toast-color control is accurate.

Some toasters now come with small electric motors that lower and raise the bread automatically. These eliminate the need to handle levers, but make sure that there is a release button so that you can, if necessary, interrupt the toasting cycle.

Crumb tray: Is it hinged or does it slide out easily for cleaning?

Handles: Are they of a non-heat-conducting material and large enough to grasp firmly?

Toaster slots: Are they large enough for the type of bread or muffins that you eat most regularly? Some units have wide slots for English muffins or thick bread. Are the coils set back so that you will not come in contact with them? Is the toast pushed up high enough for easy removal?

Switch: Toasters should have a two-pole safety switch so that they are shockproof when not working even though they are plugged into an outlet.

Base: The base should be solid, as the entire mechanism is mounted on it.

Current conductors: For added safety, the current should be carried by steel bars rather than wires, as the latter tend to flex and wear thin.

FIG. 1 This Sovereign 2-slice toaster (B112), by Toastmaster, has conveniently located controls on the front. The large lever depresses easily. The color-control dial, while small, turns easily, and the toast-release push button is located just at the

FIG. 1

bottom of the panel. It has a timer, bar construction, a 2-pole safety switch, a hinged crumb tray, and a shockproof chassis. Bakelite handles stay cool and make it easy to move the toaster when it is not in use. Power is 955 watts, 120 volts, AC only. List price is about $24 at appliance and department stores. Sears Roebuck makes a similar unit (34A6336) which costs about $16. A similar Toastmaster model, the Imperial (B122), has a motor to lower the toast.

FIG. 2 This compact Automatic Toaster (Model T15), by General Electric, browns simultaneously on both sides. It works well for breads of varying sizes, muffins, and other pastries. The small temperature control turns easily with the push of a finger to set the amount of toasting time needed. The lever is then depressed. When toasting is complete, the lever pops up, and the current goes off. The coils are well recessed in the back. The handles stay cool so that the unit can easily be moved. A hinged crumb tray underneath folds down for cleaning. List price is about $16.

FIG. 2

FIG. 3 This Deluxe Toast-R-Oven (Model T-93), by General Electric, is designed for heating, baking, and toasting. Instructions carefully tell you that it cannot be used for broiling.

This oven is compact enough to be stored at the back of the counter for quick access, leaving enough room in front of it to work on the surface top. The unit heats quickly, and the sides stay cool enough to handle while the oven is in use.

The sliding temperature controls work easily. The push-to-activate Start button depresses with light pressure, as does the Open lever. When the Open lever is depressed, the door opens, the tray slides halfway out, and the current to the oven automatically goes off. This is especially helpful if you are forgetful.

The oven area is small, 5¾ by 10 inches, so that the oven can be used for toasting 2 slices of bread, heating a few rolls, baking a meat loaf, potatoes, meat pies, small casseroles, making custards and other small items. It will not heat a frozen prepared dinner, bake a dessert pie, or a layer cake, as the depth is too narrow. List price is about $37 at houseware and appliance stores.

FIG. 3

HOT POTS (LIQUID HEATERS)

Liquid heaters bring water to a boil at the rate of about 1 cup per 1½ minutes, and hold varying amounts up to 6 cups. In addition to boiling water for tea or coffee, they can be used to heat soups, sauces, and canned vegetables, to make gelatin desserts and instant mashed potatoes, and to boil eggs.

Several brands of hot pots are on the market. Not all, however, are Underwriters' Laboratories listed, or safe. None, at present, has an On-Off switch, so any one you select must be fitted with a cord-line switch or socket switch.

Features to look for include the following:

Temperature control: Look for a unit with settings which range from Warm to Boil. Make sure that you can slide the lever quickly. This is necessary to prevent liquids from boiling over.

Handle design: Pick up the unit and make sure that your hand does not come in contact with the metal. When the unit is hot, there is no insulation to keep you from getting burned. A handle of non-heat-conducting material with a baffle along the inner side is safest.

Construction: Check to make sure the base is secure and that it will not heat up and burn a surface. Some units have a base of Bakelite or similar non-heat-conducting material. Some models are Teflon-lined for easier cleaning.

Cover: A cover is helpful, but not always necessary, as the unit is used for quick heating and not for simmering.

Plug location: Try putting in the plug. Sometimes the location of the socket makes it difficult to put the plug in. If you are using the hot pot for water only, you may not have to unplug it often. Otherwise you will want to get the plug and cord off in order to wash the pot.

FIG. 1 The Insta-Hot (Model 7796), by Regal Ware, Inc., holds from 1 to 6 cups of liquid, has graduated markings, and will boil up to 32 ounces.

The pot is of seamless aluminum construction with a Teflon interior for easy cleaning. The handle and the base are both of heat-resistant Bakelite. If you lack coordination or have loss of grasp in one or both hands, you will find that you can pick up the pot without touching the hot metal, as the handle has a Bakelite baffle along the interior side.

An automatic control adjusts to and maintains any temperature from 100° to 225°. It is marked for Warm, Hot, and Boil. However, the unit does not have an On-Off switch. We recommend that you purchase a line switch and have it installed in the cord, or that you arrange to install another type of On-Off control. Cost is about $9.50 at houseware stores and mail-order firms, including Suburbia Inc., and Darby,

FIG. 1

Inc. A line switch makes this unit safer and more convenient to use. (See pages 72 and 73.)

West Bend manufactures a similar liquid heater (3251) of lightweight aluminum construction, with a handle set far enough away from the metal base to enable a person with good grasp in one hand to pick it up safely. Cost is about $10.

ELECTRIC GRINDERS

Electric grinders can grind cooked or uncooked meats, vegetables, and fruit. The base contains the motor. The food is put into an aluminum hopper, and is forced through a fine- or coarse-grinding disk. A wooden pusher is provided. Optional attachments include vegetable slicer-shredders and sausage-stuffers.

The electric food grinder is probably most useful to the home-maker on a special diet who must have very lean ground meat, or to the woman who prefers to prepare traditional dishes from start to finish, and due to a physical disability, needs a time-saving way to prepare meat, liver, or fish.

Be sure to check on the following features—whether you can operate the On-Off switch, and whether you can put on and take off the hopper. Grinding is easy, as the revolving blades catch the food. Food grinders come with some stand mixers as an optional attachment.

FIG. 1 This Hamilton Beach Food Converter set (168) consists of a power unit with grinding and slicing accessories. The push-button controls, located on the top, are easy to manage. The aluminum hopper must be pushed into position, but releases

FIG. 1

on depression of an ejector button. The grinder parts can be handled by those with one normally functioning hand, or with two weak hands.

Cut the food in chunks before putting it in the hopper. The rotating wheel at the bottom of the hopper catches the food and pushes it through the slicing blades. A wooden pusher can be used to give an occasional assist. Cost is about $43 at appliance stores.

Rival manufactures an electric food grinder similar to the Hamilton Beach, but with no accessory parts. The release mechanism, however, is a screw-type knob which must be turned to loosen the grinding blades and hopper, and requires moderate pinch in one hand. Cost is about $30.

Serving

It's easier to get food to the table at the correct serving temperature if you use a lapboard or wheeled table. This way, you can transport more items and cut down on back-and-forth trips to the kitchen. It also helps to use serving aids that maintain food at the desired temperature, such as warming trays, warming tables on wheels, countertop heating lights, and even cold trays.

FIG. 1 A wheeled table speeds the transportation of items and gives you added stability as you walk. Look for a sturdy unit at department stores; avoid models that stress style rather than durability. The wheeled cart in this diagram is made with a fairly thick plywood top and pull-out shelf, and thick plywood sides. Surfaces are finished with a water-, stain-, and acid-resistant coating to make them easy to clean. The tops of some models have a raised metal stripping edge to prevent items from slipping off. (Plan from Occupational Therapy Service, Institute of Rehabilitation Medicine, New York University Medical Center, 400 East 34th Street, New York, New York 10016.)

FIG. 2 A basket over your arm will enable you to carry many small items, even if you are walking with a cane. Double handles help keep the basket balanced.

FIG. 3 Warming trays come in many models, from 8-inch-square units for a single casserole warmer to long buffet servers. This Salton tray (Model H-122) will hold two medium-size casseroles, and costs about $10.

FIG. 3

FIG. 1

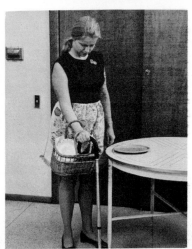

FIG. 2

FIG. 4

FIG. 4 This insulated serving dish, by Thermo Serv, consists of three pieces—a double-wall insulated lid and base and a removable aluminum liner, which can be used for baking, freezing, or chilling. The dish will keep foods hot or cold for hours, and is a help if you find serving meals a lengthy process. The unit is lightweight and handles stay cool for easy lifting or carrying. It can be washed by hand or in an automatic dishwasher. Cost is about $10. It's manufactured by the N.F.C. Engineering Company. An insulated pitcher is also available, by Thermo Serv.

Eating Aids

You'll enjoy mealtime more if you are able to handle food easily at the table. If you have trouble handling utensils because of manual disability, a simple aid may help. Most of the items shown here are commercially available.

HANDLING FOOD

FIG. 1 Lightweight forks and spoons with extra large handles make holding easier if your grasp is weak, or your fingers do not flex completely. This bamboo-handled fork is part of a set now

FIG. 1

available at import stores and general mail-order firms. Prices start at about $1.50 per place setting.

FIG. 2 You can easily build up the handle of a standard eating utensil with a foam rubber curler. The rough surface of the curler increases friction, and thus aids holding. These curlers are available at drug and variety stores for about 60¢ a set.

FIG. 2

FIG. 3 Built-up eating utensils can be purchased at self-help equipment firms. Included are built-up teaspoons, tablespoons, forks, and knives. The expandable handles shown here are from Be O/K Sales; other similar utensils are available from G. E. Miller, Rehab Aids, and J. A. Preston. Cost is $1.25 to $3 per utensil.

FIG. 3

FIG. 4 If grasp is lacking, a Universal Cuff, consisting of an elastic band with a palmar pocket, may be slipped on your hand. The palmar pocket will hold ordinary eating utensils. Each cuff is $1.50 at Bio-Tex Devices.

A similar holder with a Velcro closure adjusts to fit the hand. You may prefer it if you cannot fully extend your fingers to slip on a cuff. There's also a plastic and elastic cuff available from Be O/K Sales and other self-help firms for about $1.80.

FIG. 5 Stainless steel spring-clip holders will slip into palmar pockets of cuffs or cockup splints. The specially designed utensil is held in place by a spring clip and is angled to make it easier to handle food. Clip holders are about $4.50 each, and utensils cost $2.50 each. A cockup splint with a palmar pocket is about $7. All are from Bio-Tex.

FIG. 6 A swivel spoon rotates to keep the bowl of the spoon level as you lift it to your mouth. It's especially helpful if you have poor coordination or difficulty rotating your forearm. Cost of a large-handled utensil is about $2.40 to $3.50 per utensil from Be O/K Sales, G. E. Miller, Rehab Aids, and J. A. Preston.

The adjustable swivel spoon shown here has a flat handle to fit into the pocket of a utensil-holder cuff. It's available from Be O/K Sales.

FIG. 7 If you have difficulty reaching your mouth due to arthritis or other conditions that limit shoulder or elbow movement, one solution is a lengthened eating utensil. Extension units with

FIG. 4

FIG. 5

FIG. 6

FIG. 7

built-up handles are carried by Be O/K Sales and G. E. Miller, and cost about $2.50 to $4 each.

This extended handle fits into the palmar pocket of a Universal Cuff and is also available from Be O/K Sales and G. E. Miller.

FIG. 8 By using a rocker knife, you can cut meat and other foods with one hand. As you rock the handle up and down several times, the sharp, curved blade slices through the food. Rocker knives cost about $3.75 to $4.50 each from self-help firms, including G. E. Miller, Be O/K Sales, Rehab Aids, Cleo Living Aids, and J. A. Preston, and are manufactured by the Lamson and Goodnow Manufacturing Company.

FIG. 9 A small Danish sandwich board with a raised ledge makes spreading bread easier. Select an attractive ¼-inch-thick piece of hardwood and finish it with salad oil. (See page 202.)

FIG. 10 When it's difficult to pick up food with a spoon or fork, a plate guard provides a stable area to push against, and may be especially useful during the learning stage. This unit from Be O/K Sales comes in two sizes to clip onto dinner or

FIG. 8

FIG. 9

FIG. 10

dessert plates. The small size guard for 6- to 8-inch plates costs about $4.50; the large guard for 9- to 11-inch plates is $4.80. Other plate guards, some with bulldog clips, are distributed by Cleo Living Aids, G. E. Miller, and Rehab Aids.

FIG. 11 If weak grasp or poor coordination makes it difficult for you to hold a sandwich, or if arthritis or other conditions cause difficulties in reaching your mouth, a sandwich or hand food holder is useful. The holder shown here is made from a pair of 8-inch-long kitchen utility tongs. A small piece of Velcro holds the handles together and maintains pressure on the sandwich. If you wish, you can build up the tops of the tongs with a small metal plate on each side, to further stabilize the food.

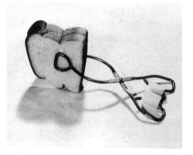

FIG. 11

HANDLING LIQUIDS

FIG. 12

FIG. 12 Stretch-knit coasters slip onto a glass to provide a more secure grasping area. Terry jackets come in sets of 6 from gift and houseware stores, or write the Hi-Jac Corporation.

A bathtub safety tread spiraled around a glass also increases friction for safer holding. Adhesive-backed treads are sold by houseware and department stores.

FIG. 13 If you have marked weakness or poor coordination of the upper extremities, it's easier to sip liquids through a long straw, instead of trying to pick up a glass. Eighteen-inch-long Plexiglas or polyethylene reusable straws are available through hospital-supply houses and self-help equipment firms, including Rehab Aids and Be O/K Sales. Cost is about $1.30 to $1.80 per package of 5, depending on hole size (⅛ to ¼ inch). Straws may also be cut from surgical tubing and bent to the desired angle. A small bulldog clip or pencil clip will secure the straw to the side of your glass.

If you're able to lift a cup or glass, but still need a straw to drink more easily, you may prefer a shorter straw. Flex-Straws have a spiral corrugation so that they can be bent to stay in any position. A high-temperature-resistant coating makes this paper straw adaptable for hot and cold drinks. Flexible plastic straws, also from Flex-Straw, are carried by local grocery stores and hospital-supply houses.

FIG. 14 If you have loss of grasp, this glass-holder handle will permit you to lift a tumbler safely to your mouth. The metal ring is lined with rubber. Several models are available from self-help firms, including Be O/K Sales, Rehab Aids, J. A. Preston, and G. E. Miller. Cost is about $2 to $3 each.

FIG. 15 This Mac Mug has a molded plastic handle that's easy to pick up with a variety of grasping patterns. Cost is about $1.20 for a package of 2 from department stores, Be O/K Sales, or Deka Plastics.

FIG. 14

FIG. 13

FIG. 15

FIG. 16 This Tommee Tippee cup, by Westland Plastics, Inc. (Model No. WP123), was originally designed to train children to drink from a cup. However, it's also been useful to older children and adults who have difficulty learning to swallow after an injury, or who have very poor coordination. The unbreakable plastic cup has a spout and a "see thru" cover. The curved base is weighted to prevent tipping. Cost is about $1 at department stores.

FIG. 17 This Wonder-Flo vacuum cup is useful if you're confined to bed and must lie flat on your back or on your side. A special spout prevents spilling—the flow stops when you stop sucking. You can increase the flow of liquids by pressing on the rubber knob. You can drink tea or fruit juices or even thick liquids like pureed soup from this 8-ounce cup, which may be sterilized after use. Cost is about $1.75 from hospital-supply and self-help equipment firms. Be O/K Sales carries a modified Wonder-Flo cup with double handles, designed for the person who can sit up but has very weak upper extremities. Cost is about $3.30 per cup.

FIG. 16   FIG. 17

Clean-Up

Dishwashing is a necessary mealtime chore. Often, we can enlist the family's help, but when this is not practical or possible, several techniques may make the job easier for you.

You can wash dishes from a sitting position, using a high chair, a standard kitchen chair, a glider chair, or a wheelchair. Add a cushion to the seat if reaching is difficult. If you have a cabinet under the sink, open its doors and extend your feet into the cabinet area. If you use a wheelchair, adaption of the entire sink area is desirable. (See suggestions under Kitchen Planning.)

The first step in simplifying kitchen clean-up is to think ahead. Careful planning will enable you to use a minimum number of utensils and dishes, and to avoid scrubbing as much as possible.

To eliminate the "middleman" serving dish, use oven-to-table ware, or serve directly from the pot.

Mix ingredients right in a casserole and you won't have to wash an extra bowl.

Nonstick pans rinse clean without scrubbing. Protect them by using only recommended products for cleaning.

Line pans with foil when baking, cooking, or roasting or broiling meat or fish (but don't line the rack). Afterward, throw away the foil, and your pan will need little washing.

Pre-shaped foil pans come in various sizes for cakes, casseroles, pies, and other foods. The extra cost of throw-away units is more than compensated for in terms of the free time and energy you gain from using them.

Immersible bags leave your pots clean. Many frozen main dishes and vegetables are packaged this way. When you're cooking "double batches," it's a good idea to pack your own extra meals in plastic bags. (See page 55.)

Judicious use of paper towels, plastic wrap, waxed paper, and foil saves cleaning up.

So you've thought ahead, and done all the things mentioned above, and you still have dirty dishes waiting. Let's proceed to cut the job down to size.

Soak all dirty utensils and pans immediately after use. Fill pans used for starchy foods or eggs with cold water, those used for greasy foods with hot water. While you eat, utensils and pans can bathe in hot water and detergent, so that when the meal is finished there's hardly a pot left to scrub.

Organize the items to be washed. A dishwasher, if you have or can afford one, cuts out almost all of the next steps. It's more sanitary than handwashing, and also stores dishes until you're ready to set the table again.

Your work area should be set up to permit a coordinated flow of activity from left to right or vice versa, i.e., soiled dishes, wash water, rinse water (or spray), and drying rack. If you're working with one hand, the rinse water and drying rack should be adjacent to your good hand.

Bring dishes to and from the work area on a wheeled cart, and return them to storage areas on the same cart. If you're in a wheel-chair, a lapboard will serve the purpose. (See pages 28 to 29.)

Rinse dishes well once they're washed and let them dry in the dish drainer. Only sterling, silver-plate, and cast-iron items need to be dried with a towel.

FIG. 1 To determine if your sink is a comfortable depth for you, stretch the palms of your hands as far as you can toward the bottom of the sink, without leaning forward. If you can't reach the bottom, add a simple rack. The rack shown here is made from the ends of an orange crate, but you can use any ¾-inch-thick wood. The grain should run lengthwise. Use thinner wood across the top, but be sure it's strong enough to support the dishpan. Two nails or screws fasten the ends of the slats to the upright pieces. A water-resistant finish prevents the wood from getting water-soaked.

FIG. 1

FIG. 2 Sinks come in many depths. If you're planning to do some kitchen remodeling and are confined to a wheelchair, a 5½-inch-deep sink set in a 31-inch-high counter will allow you to roll under the sink far enough to use it comfortably. (If you have very long legs and your knees come up high, you can purchase a 4-inch-deep sink.) Stainless steel sinks in various depths and styles are made by several manufacturers including Eljer and American Standard. Make sure the pipes are covered or wrapped to prevent burning your legs.

The Bluette Neoprene gloves worn by this homemaker are especially helpful when you have disturbance of sensation in your hands, or when hands are weak and coordination is poor. The Neoprene insulates your hands against hot water, and the nonslip grip helps you hold wet dishes firmly. A cotton-knit lining allows you to slip the gloves on without difficulty. Bluette gloves may be washed in an automatic machine. They're made by the Pioneer Rubber Company and come in three sizes: small, medium, and large. Cost is about $1.90 at houseware and department stores. A single glove replacement comes with your first pair, a great help to those who are limited to the use of one hand.

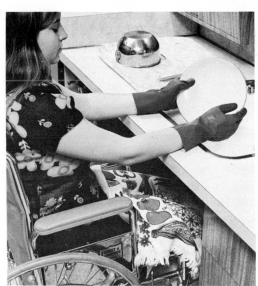

FIG. 2

FIG. 3 If you have difficulty reaching faucets, or if the sensation in your hands is impaired, so that it's not advisable to touch hot faucet handles, you'll find an S-shaped closet hook on the end of a dowel or aluminum rod useful.

FIG. 3

FIG. 4 If you have arthritis or weakness in the upper extremities, faucet openers of wood with built-up or extended handles will provide more leverage for turning.

FIG. 4

FIG. 5 Easy-to-operate, single-handle controls may be installed. These operate on a single ball-bearing and move from On to Off and from Hot to Cold with just the push of your hand. Manufacturers include American Standard, Delta, Elkay, and Eljer.

A rubber mat at the bottom of the dishpan or sink helps prevent breakage and keeps dishes from slipping while you scrub. Rubber mats come in various styles from a number of

FIG. 5

manufacturers. Rubbermaid makes rubber sink divider mats as well.

To stabilize a pan for scouring, place a sponge cloth under it and wedge it in a corner of the sink. A suction-based brush is good for scrubbing stubborn foods off tableware, plates, and other utensils. Cost is about $1 from self-help equipment firms, including Be O/K Sales and G. E. Miller, or write the Anchor Brush Company. Larger suction-based brushes for washing glasses are available from restaurant suppliers, including the National Brush Company. However, glasses can usually be soaked and rinsed clean without scrubbing.

FIG. 6 If weak hands make grasping difficult, or if your fingers must be kept extended while you work (as in arthritis), you may find a large sponge easier to scrub with than a smaller, more flexible pad or cloth. Several types of cellulose sponges,

FIG. 6

bonded to sturdy nylon scrubbers, are now available. Choose different sponges for different tasks, depending on the degree of abrasiveness required. For example, you might want to use a cookware sponge to clean nonstick-coated utensils, a kitchen sponge for heavy-duty scouring of pots and grills, a tub-and-sink sponge, and a utility sponge for walls, woodwork, and outdoor grills. Sponge/Scrubber, by E. I. DuPont de Nemours, is fine for the kitchen and costs about 40¢. Similar Scotch-Brite Scrub 'n Sponges are available at grocery and variety stores for 30¢ to 80¢ each, and are made by Minnesota Mining and Manufacturing Company.

FIG. 7 Rinsing dishes and letting them dry in the air is much easier and more sanitary than wiping them. A spray hose greatly simplifies the rinsing process. If you don't have a spray hose, use a lightweight plastic decanter with a single handle to pour water over the dishes.

If you have loss of sensation in your hands, *never* immerse dishes in hot water to rinse them; either use a spray hose or a plastic decanter.

To dry silverware, use a large, absorbent terrycloth dish towel. If you're seated and using one hand, put the towel in your lap and bring the utensil to your lap to be dried. If you work with one hand while standing, use the counter to support the utensil and the towel.

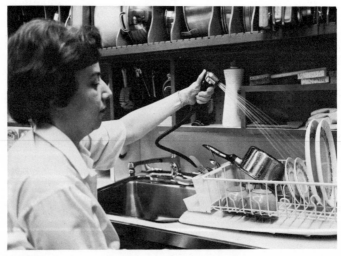

FIG. 7

FIG. 8 PAM spray-on pure vegetable coating helps reduce clean-up by preventing food from sticking to surfaces. When released from the aerosol container, this soybean derivative forms a tough, clear, tasteless shield that is not absorbed by food and to which food will not stick. PAM adds no fat or calories. Look for it in the cooking oil section of your supermarket. It's made by Gibraltar Industries, Inc.

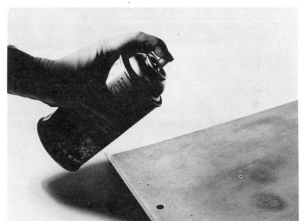

FIG. 8

Shopping

Planning ahead will help make your shopping trips easier and more · fun. Keep a pad handy in the kitchen. List the items you need, but leave enough time when shopping to wander occasionally and look at the new convenience foods on your grocer's shelves.

Carrying heavy packages may be difficult or impossible. If, for example, you have arthritis, you should avoid putting stress on the joints. Having foods delivered is one solution. Another is to arrange to shop at a place where someone will load the bags into your car. Plan to have someone at home unload them when you reach there. If food cannot be delivered promptly, have refrigerated items packed separately and take them home yourself. Some homemakers carry an inexpensive insulated picnic refrigerator in the car to store items during extended periods.

For light shopping trips, several simple aids may help. A large, over-the-shoulder bag transfers the weight of small purchases from the hands and arms to the trunk and shoulder. Several styles are available at department stores and airline companies. When shopping in a wheelchair, use your lapboard to carry a generous supply of groceries.

FIG. 1 This wheeled shopping cart folds when not in use and can be carried like a pocketbook. It holds the equivalent of two large shopping bags, and costs about $7 at department stores. Folding metal carts cost about $5 to $9 at department stores. Look for a unit with sturdy wheels.

FIG. 1

Nutrition—Menus

Good nutrition is essential to good health. Only by consuming the proper amounts and kinds of foods will our bodies function at their peak. A variety of foods can easily be selected from fresh, frozen, canned, and dehydrated products found in supermarkets and grocery stores. If a little care is taken in planning and preparing meals, all the essential nutrients can be obtained economically.

All through life we need the same basic nutrients. However, our caloric needs decrease as we grow older and when we are less active. Thus, it is especially important at this time to maintain variety in our meals. Often there's a tendency to select foods that are not well balanced in that they do not supply enough proteins, vitamins, and minerals in relation to our decreased caloric needs. In some cases, a special diet may be necessary. This should always be recommended by a physician. Sources of information on planning special diets are given at the end of this chapter.

A variety of foods will usually provide the proper amount and balance of nutrients at the least cost, as well as give the greatest enjoyment. The recipes in this book are designed to help you plan and serve nutritious meals. You will enjoy them more and they will probably do you more good if you eat in a leisurely fashion and in pleasant surroundings.

As you probably know, foods supply nutrients which are classified as proteins, carbohydrates, fats, minerals, and vitamins. Fiber is a part of food that cannot be digested; though not a nutrient, it is usually desirable in the diet to provide bulk. Also, it is important that you drink enough liquids.

You'll want to remember the following five kinds of nutrients (which include some 50 specific ones) required for proper body function. The nutrients perform different roles in the body.

Proteins are composed of building blocks called amino acids. They are used to build, maintain, and repair body tissues.

Carbohydrates serve as sources of energy for work and maintenance of body temperature. Starches and sugars fall in this classification.

Fats also serve as primary sources of energy and contain a little more than twice the number of calories in carbohydrates. Some fats contain other essential nutrients.

Minerals are necessary for the formation of teeth, bone, and red blood cells. They are also required for many other vital body functions.

Vitamins have many different roles. They are necessary for the proper utilization of foods and the healthy functioning of the body.

The functions of all the nutrients are interrelated. One nutrient cannot do its job properly without all the others being present. For example, the proteins in cereal are more nutritious if they are consumed with milk. No one food contains all the essential nutrients in proper balance except in the case of mother's milk for newborn infants. Thus, we need an assortment of foods at every meal.

BASIC FOUR FOODS

Foods have been placed into four different groups to help you plan nutritious meals. Unless you are on a special diet, foods should be selected from the following food groups:

Meat Group: Eat two servings every day. A serving is two or three ounces of meat, poultry, or fish, without bone or fat. You may substitute two eggs or a cup of dried peas or beans for one of your meat servings.

Bread-Cereal Group: Each day include four servings of enriched or whole grain breads and cereals in your meals. A serving is one slice of bread, three-quarters of a cup of ready-to-eat cereal, or one-half of a cup of cooked cereal, macaroni, noodles, rice, or spaghetti.

Milk Group: Serve milk every day. Adults should have one to two glasses.

Children need two to four glasses. You can use whole milk, skim milk, evaporated or dry milk, or buttermilk. You can substitute one ounce of cheese or a serving of ice cream for a glass of milk.

Vegetable-Fruit Group: Everyone should have four or more servings each day. One serving should be a citrus fruit or tomato for vitamin C. At least four times a week a dark green or deep yellow vegetable or fruit should be served for vitamin A. A serving is one-half cup of vegetables or fruit.

The amount of food needed depends on your age, sex, and activity. A good rule to follow is to eat a sufficient quantity to achieve proper weight. If you are slightly overweight and must lose a few pounds, continue to eat a variety of foods but reduce the size of servings. Of course, if you need to gain a little weight, serve slightly larger portions. Your doctor should advise you as to the necessity of changing your weight.

Sometimes diets are not balanced. This is often due to one or more of the following reasons: (1) skipping breakfast which leads to irregular eating habits; (2) eating foods which have too many calories in relation to essential nutrients; (3) eating meals that lack variety; (4) eating food improperly prepared. Some vitamins and minerals are soluble in water, so cook with as little water as possible. Also, some vitamins are destroyed by heating, so foods should not be overcooked.

The four food groups discussed above should merely serve as a guide for meal planning. To round out meals and to satisfy the appetite, other foods and seasonings may usually be added. Some of these are butter, margarine, fats, oils, sugar and other sweets. To translate the food found in the four food groups into appetizing meals, refer to the Basic Meal Plan on page 140. You will see how the four food groups fit into this basic pattern. Then continue on to the sample menus that follow. These will show you how, with specific recipes, the foods can be fitted into a meal plan so that you and your family are assured of getting the food you need for a nutritious, well-balanced diet.

Many families eat their big meal at noon. If you are one of these, use the dinner menu at noontime and the lunch menu for your evening meal.

Foods from the four food groups are often eaten in combination. For example, in Menu 3, the dinner main dish, Spanish Rice, contains beef from the Meat Group, rice from the Bread-Cereal Group and vegetables from the Vegetable-Fruit Group. When you serve a mixed dish of this sort, you will have satisfied part of the requirements of three food groups.

Please note that each of the breakfast menus contains a protein food (meat or egg), because many nutritionists recommend this as well as protein for lunch and dinner. Or if you have cereal and milk, these two foods in combination make a complete protein source.

BASIC MEAL PLAN

Bread-Cereal Group	Meat Group	Vegetable-Fruit Group	Milk Group
4 servings per day	2 servings per day	4 servings per day	1 to 2 glasses— Adults 2 to 4 glasses— Children Teens

BREAKFAST

Toast or Roll and/or Cereal	Meat or Eggs	Fruit or Juice (citrus or tomato)	Milk

LUNCH

Bread or Macaroni	Meat or Beans or Peanut Butter	Vegetables and/or Fruit	Milk or Ice Cream, or Cottage Cheese

DINNER

Spaghetti or Rice or Noodles and/or Bread	Meat or Fish or Chicken or Shellfish	Vegetables and/or Fruit	Milk or Ice Cream, or Cheese

Extras: Tea, coffee, butter or margarine, honey, jelly, salad dressings.

MENU 1

BREAKFAST
V-8 Cocktail Vegetable Juice
Instant Oatmeal with Raisins   Milk
Toasted Wheat Germ or Whole Wheat Bread   Butter or Margarine
Coffee, Tea, or Milk

LUNCH
Creamed Chipped Beef
on Toast
Carrot and Celery Sticks
Fresh Fruit
Coffee, Tea, or Milk

DINNER
Glorified Chicken*
Baked Potato   Mixed Vegetables
Cranberry Orange Salad on Lettuce*
Biscuits   Butter or Margarine
Midnight Bavarian Cream*
Coffee, Tea, or Milk

* Recipe given in book.

MENU 2

BREAKFAST
Half Grapefruit
Frozen Breakfast: Scrambled Eggs; Sausage Patty;
Country-Style Fried Potatoes
Toast   Butter or Margarine
Coffee, Tea, or Milk

LUNCH
Tomato Soup
Opened-Faced Grilled Cheese Sandwich
Pickles and Radishes
Cookies
Coffee, Tea, or Milk

DINNER
Saucy Fish Skillet Favorite*
Parslied Rice   Broccoli
Crisp Green Salad
Corn Muffins   Butter or Margarine
Baked Fruit Strudel (Frozen)
Coffee, Tea, or Milk

* Recipe given in book.

MENU 3

BREAKFAST
Sliced Banana in Orange Juice
Ready-to-Eat Cereal   Milk
English Muffin   Butter or Margarine
Coffee, Tea, or Milk

LUNCH
Chicken Salad Sandwich*
Rice Pudding or
Fresh Fruit
Coffee, Tea, or Milk

DINNER
Spanish Rice*
Marinated Green Bean Salad
Italian Bread   Butter or Margarine
Baked Apple*
Coffee, Tea, or Milk

*Recipe given in book.

SENSIBLE SNACKING

You usually put on extra pounds by consuming foods which have a high caloric content and fall outside the Basic Four Food Groups. If you like to snack, choose foods that are low in calories, such as celery or carrot sticks, one or two crackers, vegetable or fruit juices, fruit-flavored gelatin, beef broth or consommé, nonfat milk or fresh fruit. A calorie table will help you select healthful snacks.

SPECIAL DIETS

Although the techniques in this book are designed to help the home-maker manage more easily in her kitchen, the recipes and menus are not planned for the person on a special diet. There are, however, several places where you can get information and help.

Your physician: If your doctor recommends a special diet to you and gives you a general plan, ask him for specifics. You'll want to know which foods you can eat and which you cannot, and the daily amounts of each. He may be able to recommend printed material, including recipes, for your diet. If he's connected with a hospital, he may arrange an interview for you with the hospital dietitian to help you with menu-planning. Or he may suggest a dietetic consulting service in your area of the country. A few cities now have a

Dial-A-Dietitian telephone service, run by the American Dietetic Association.

The dietitian: If you're given a diet during your stay in the hospital, then you, the dietitian, and the person who does the cooking at home should sit down before you leave to make sure you completely understand the diet.

Other agencies: County extension services are usually staffed with home economists who can answer questions on special diets or recommend available services. Look under Home Economics Extension Service, or Extension Service in your phone book. The local Department of Health or Home Nursing Service have dietitians and nutritionists who can assist. In some cities there is even a "Meals on Wheels" program which will bring food to your home when you are bedridden. The home economics teacher in your local school can often assist. Utility companies usually have home economists on their staffs who are glad to help.

Books and printed information: Local bookstores have suitable books on diet planning, or will order them for you. Your doctor, dietitian, or health agencies can suggest specific recommended titles. Many of these books are available in inexpensive paperbacks. The federal government also publishes several books to help homemakers with special meal planning.

Organizations concerned with health problems publish materials, too. These include: The American Diabetes Association, the Allergy Foundation of America, and The American Heart Association. (Addresses are given under sources on pages 226 to 228.) Before writing the national office, check your phone book for a local chapter in the nearest metropolitan area to you.

Major food companies often have booklets and information about their products in relation to special diets. Write to the Consumer Services Department. The address of the company is on the product label.

Several magazines, notably *Good Housekeeping,* have booklets available with information and recipes for special diets.

Shopping has become easier and more exciting for the individual on a special diet. Many large supermarkets carry an extensive variety of dietetic foods. If you have any doubts about the product being right for your diet, ask your physician first. (Incidentally, "dietetic" foods are not necessarily low calorie.)

Convenience Foods

Today's good cooks can create exciting meals for the family in less time than it took grandmother to heat the stove. Now it's possible for her to buy foods—from appetizers to desserts—with every degree of convenience built into them.

Consider beef stew, for example. You can make your own with meat cubed by the butcher and a package of frozen "stew" vegetables, or buy savory canned beef stew to heat and serve. In the frozen foods counter at the market, you'll find packaged fried chicken that only needs to be heated in the oven. Nearby are frozen, 3-course dinners to heat and eat.

In the dairy case are cubed, grated, and sliced cheeses to help you season dishes or to use in hot and cold sandwiches.

Every day, new canned products with more variety and better flavor are added to the grocery shelf. Look for condensed soups to use in lunches or as sauces for main dishes. You'll also find canned meats, chicken, and fish; canned spaghetti, gravies, and even dessert puddings.

In addition to cake, muffin, hot roll, corn bread, and coffee-cake mixes, you can now buy mixes for pudding cakes, upside-down cakes, and special desserts like Boston cream pie.

Convenience foods, whether partially or fully prepared, mean a great saving for you in time and effort. Many prepared foods, like frozen orange juice concentrate, soups, cake and dessert mixes, and many frozen and canned vegetables and fruits, actually cost the same or less than homemade.

Most convenience foods are made from vegetables and other ingredients at the peak of their quality, and are processed to preserve freshness, flavor, and food value. Thus, if you serve a good variety of foods and follow the meal plan given in the Nutrition section (see pages 136 to 144), you can be assured that you and your family are eating a well-balanced diet. When reading labels, remember that the law requires food companies to list all the ingredients in a product, with the ingredient containing the greatest quantity or amount listed first, and so on.

BE CREATIVE WITH CONVENIENCE FOODS

It's fun to cook with convenience foods when you add your own special touches. All the done-for-you steps leave you more time to dress up a product. For example, if you use instant mashed potatoes, you can add variety by folding in shredded Cheddar cheese or grated Parmesan cheese. Top a favorite meat casserole with fluffs of instant mashed potatoes during the last few minutes of baking.

When you use canned puddings, add toppings for interest. Crown rice pudding with spoonfuls of canned cherry pie filling. Garnish chocolate pudding with toasted coconut or peanuts.

CONVENIENCE FOODS YOU'LL WANT TO TRY

Here's a partial list of convenience foods on the market. You're probably familiar with many of them, but others may suggest new possibilities to you. Many of these staple convenience foods you'll want to keep on hand for times when bad weather keeps you from shopping or when company drops in unexpectedly. With these foods in the freezer and on the shelf, you can always serve appetizing meals to your family or to guests with a minimum of time and effort.

BREAKFAST ITEMS

canned and frozen fruit juices; tomato and mixed vegetable juices
ready-to-eat and quick-cooking cereals
frozen breakfasts (heat and serve)
instant coffee and tea

SOUPS

ready-to-serve, condensed, frozen and dehydrated varieties (for lunches and sauces)

Prepared Main Dishes and Dinners (heat and serve)

frozen dinners
frozen pouch items (individual servings)
frozen tray items (individual servings)
frozen meat pies (8-ounce or 1-pound deep-dish size)
canned and frozen meat, fish, shellfish, and poultry
canned stews, beans, and spaghetti products

Vegetables, Rice, and Pastas

canned and frozen vegetables: plain, with butter sauce, and with seasoned
    sauce or glaze
frozen potatoes: french fries, au gratin, puffs, cut for hashed brown
instant potato mixes: mashed, scalloped, au gratin, potato pancakes
quick-cooking rice and seasoned rice
packaged noodles with seasonings or sauce

Salad Items

canned potato, fruit, and mixed bean salad
bottled salad dressings
salad dressing mixes

Breads

ready-to-eat and frozen breads, rolls, coffee cakes, waffles, pancakes, and
    French toast
brown-and-serve rolls and bread
refrigerated doughs for rolls, biscuits, and coffee cakes
mixes: hot rolls, muffins, popovers, coffee cakes, breads, biscuits, and
    pancakes

Desserts

frozen cakes
frozen unbaked fruit turnovers, strudels, and tarts
frozen puddings and whipped toppings
mixes for custards, pies, cakes, frostings, puddings, toppings, cookies, and
    brownies
prepared and frozen pie crusts, regular and graham cracker
canned puddings, fruits, and pie fillings

Seasonings and Cooking Ingredients

instant flour
instant nonfat dry milk, canned evaporated and sweetened condensed milk
shredded, grated, and sliced cheese
frozen chopped onion and green pepper

instant minced onion
dried celery, parsley, green pepper flakes and chives
onion and garlic powder
grated dried lemon and orange peel
sauce mixes
canned gravies and sauces

ELIMINATE FOOD PREPARATION STEPS

In the recipe section, you will find many kitchen-tested recipes that are easy to prepare. However, you probably have favorite recipes that are old standbys, as well as new ideas you want to try. You can adapt recipes for easier preparation by substituting convenience foods for items that require chopping, cutting, or shredding. Here are some helpful substitutions:

For ¼ cup chopped fresh or frozen onion, substitute 1 tablespoon dried onion flakes or 1 tablespoon instant minced onion or 1 teaspoon onion powder.
For ¼ cup chopped fresh or frozen green pepper, substitute 1 tablespoon dried sweet pepper flakes.
For ½ medium stalk celery, substitute 1 tablespoon dried celery flakes.

A rule of thumb to follow when using dried onion flakes, pepper flakes, and celery flakes: in foods that require a short cooking time of less than 10 minutes and/or have a low liquid content, reconstitute these products according to package directions before using them.

For 1 strip of cooked bacon, substitute 1 tablespoon bacon-flavored bits.
For 1 cup diced, cooked chicken, substitute 1 can (5 ounces) boned chicken.
For 1½ cups cheese sauce, substitute 1 can (11 ounces) condensed Cheddar cheese soup plus ¼ cup milk (eliminate salt in the recipe).

Hints on Meal Planning

Some basic planning and energy-saving techniques will make meal preparation easier and less rushed.

Once a week, write down the heavier tasks that must be done and make a schedule spreading them out over the week.

Wherever possible, enlist team support from the family. If necessary, occasionally get outside help.

Set up a schedule that allows you adequate time to prepare meals, with time to rest before you serve the meals.

Before beginning any task, organize. Get everything together you need to make a meat loaf, or to bake a cake. Concentrate on that one task, then clean up and proceed to the next.

Eliminate! Why spend precious time and energy on tasks that don't have to be done. Let dishes drain dry instead of wiping them. Use ready-cut onions and other foods instead of peeling, chopping, and slicing them. Fruits served in their skins make a delicious, healthful dessert as well as a handsome table decoration.

Reduce every task to its essentials. Eliminate unnecessary lifting. It saves energy and is also safer. Slide objects along counters and tables whenever possible, rather than lifting. Get wheels, and roll items on a wheeled cart rather than carrying them. One trip with a cart can equal ten journeys without.

Double up! When making a casserole or meat loaf, make a double recipe. Freeze the second, and then glow over the fact that you don't have to prepare (and clean up) twice.

Simplified Measures

Dash	less than ⅛ teaspoon
3 teaspoons	1 tablespoon
1 cup	½ pint
2 cups	1 pint

2 pints	1 quart
4 quarts	1 gallon
4 tablespoons	¼ cup
5⅓ tablespoons	⅓ cup
8 tablespoons	½ cup
10⅔ tablespoons	⅔ cup
12 tablespoons	¾ cup
16 tablespoons	1 cup

Measuring butter or margarine is very simple if you buy ¼-pound sticks.

1 stick equals *¼ pound, ½ cup, 8 tablespoons* (tbsp) or *24 teaspoons* (tsp).

To measure a fraction of ½ a cup, cut through the stick, as shown in the diagram, at the correct point.

¼-pound stick of butter		
½ cup	¼ cup	⅛ cup
8 tablespoons	4 tablespoons	2 tablespoons
24 teaspoons	12 teaspoons	6 teaspoons

1 average lemon equals 3 tablespoons of bottled juice, and 1 tablespoon of rind. 1 average orange has ⅓ to ½ cup of juice, and 2 tablespoons of rind.

CAN SIZES

8 ounces	1 cup
Picnic	1¼ cups
No. 300	1¾ cups
No. 303	2 cups
No. 2	2½ cups
No. 2½	3½ cups
No. 3	5¾ cups

Main Dishes—Opening Containers

The ZIP-CUT BOX OPENER (C78KP), by Ekco, opens frozen food packages and other boxes. The sharp cutting edge lies under a protective guard and is designed to cut only the wrapper and not the contents. To use, rest the blade guard on the top of the package, push the blade into the package, and cut around the edge until you have the desired opening.

If you have the use of only one hand, stabilize the container in a drawer or on a sponge cloth while cutting around the box. If you have loss of power in both hands, slip the box opener into an elastic cuff. (See page 124.) Price is about 40¢ at variety stores.

QUICK COTTAGE POTATO PUFF

4 servings of packaged, instant mashed potatoes
½ cup small-curd, cream-style cottage cheese

⅛ teaspoon onion powder
paprika

Prepare potatoes as directed on package, adding cheese and onion powder. Sprinkle with paprika. *Makes 2 servings as a main dish.*

SPINACH NOODLE CASSEROLE

1 can (10½ ounces) condensed cream of mushroom soup
½ cup milk
⅛ teaspoon ground nutmeg

2 packages (10 ounces each) frozen chopped spinach, cooked and drained
2 cups cooked noodles
1 cup shredded process cheese

Blend soup, milk, and nutmeg. In a 1½-quart casserole, arrange layers of spinach, noodles, soup mixture, and cheese. Bake at 350° for 30 minutes or until hot. *Makes 2 to 3 servings.*

Sliced Cheese: Substitute 4 slices (4 ounces) American cheese for shredded cheese. Proceed as above.

The HANDY KNIFE (C33) by Hyde Tools is designed for cutting linoleum as well as opening boxes. A sharp, hooked blade of carbon steel cuts through cardboard, while the large handle provides a built-up grasping area for those with moderate weakness of the hands. Cost is about $1.30 at hardware stores.

BAKED CHICKEN AND NOODLES

1 can (10½ ounces) condensed cream of mushroom soup*
½ cup milk
2 cups cooked noodles
1 can (5 ounces) boned chicken or turkey, with broth

2 tablespoons chopped pimiento
1 tablespoon chopped parsley
2 tablespoons buttered bread crumbs

Empty contents of soup can into a 1½-quart casserole and stir until smooth. Gradually add milk. Mix in noodles, chicken, pimiento, and parsley. Top with buttered bread crumbs. Bake at 350° for 30 minutes. *Makes 4 servings.*

*Or substitute cream of celery, Cheddar cheese, or cream of chicken soup.

ZIP-CUT BOX OPENER   HANDY KNIFE

Pastas, noodles, and instant potatoes come in a wide variety of packages to add interest to everyday meals.

When your fingers are weak, or you need to avoid stress (as in arthritis), you may be unable to tear a box open. Instead, lay the box on its side and release the top with a sharp, serrated knife. If you are using only one hand, put the box on a sponge cloth to stabilize it.

The STANLEY UTILITY KNIFE (No. 99) has an adjustable retractable blade, that locks in three positions for the appropriate cutting depth. You'll probably find that you prefer the smallest extension, which is designed to open cartons without damaging the contents. Intermediate and fully extended positions are used for heavy-duty cutting jobs.

The light aluminum body is large enough to permit a secure grasp. A ridged button on top of the knife retracts the blade quickly when pushed with the thumb or the heel of the hand. Cost is about $1.70 at hardware stores.

To increase the size of a spout in the side of a box, first release the tab with a knife, then use both hands to squeeze the sides of the box together. This will make the top arch up, leaving a wider hole.

MACARONI AND CHEESE (Stove-Top)

¼ cup chopped onion (frozen or fresh) or 1 teaspoon onion powder
1 tablespoon butter or margarine

1 can (10¾ ounces) condensed Cheddar cheese soup
½ cup milk
3 cups drained cooked macaroni (about 8 ounces uncooked)

Cook onion in butter until tender. (If using onion powder, mix in with soup and omit butter.) Blend in soup; gradually add milk. Heat, stirring often. Mix in macaroni. Heat, stirring. *Makes 4 servings.*

STANLEY UTILITY KNIFE

FETTUCINI

1 can (10½ ounces) condensed cream of mushroom soup
¾ cup milk
½ cup grated Parmesan cheese

3 cups cooked hot noodles (about 8 ounces)
4 tablespoons butter or margarine

In large saucepan, stir soup until smooth. Blend in milk and cheese. Heat slowly, stirring occasionally. Just before serving, toss hot noodles with butter. Combine with soup mixture. Serve with additional cheese. *Makes 4 servings.*

If you have a weak grasp that prevents you from using a knife with one hand, try both hands for greater stability. This small knife (STAINLESS STEEL UTILITY KNIFE, No. G847WP, by Ekco, about 50¢) has a sharp point and a scalloped, serrated blade that easily pierces and cuts open a plastic pouch.

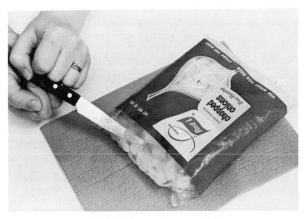

STAINLESS STEEL UTILITY KNIFE

Whether you're cutting with one or both hands, it helps to put a cellulose sponge cloth under the bag to keep it from slipping. These cloths are absorbent and easy to clean, and can be boiled to sterilize. They are manufactured by the American Sponge and Chamois Company, Inc., and E. I. DuPont de Nemours and Company, Inc., and cost about 30¢ at grocery and variety stores.

SPANISH RICE

1 pound ground beef
½ cup chopped onion (fresh
   or frozen) or 2 teaspoons
   onion powder
⅓ cup chopped green pepper
   (fresh or frozen)
1 large clove garlic, minced,
   or ½ teaspoon garlic powder

1 can (10¾ ounces) condensed
   tomato soup
1 cup water
½ cup packaged, quick-cooking
   rice, uncooked*
½ teaspoon salt
2 teaspoons Worcestershire sauce
generous dash of pepper

In skillet, brown beef and cook onion, green pepper, and garlic until vegetables are tender. Remove excess fat. Add remaining ingredients. Bring to a boil. Cover; cook over low heat 15 minutes or until rice is tender. Stir now and then. *Makes 4 servings.*

* Regular rice. Or substitute ⅓ cup raw rice. Proceed as above, cooking over low heat 30 minutes or until rice is tender. If necessary, add more liquid during cooking.

To open a heated, immersible pouch of food with one or two hands, place the pouch in a shallow serving dish and cut across the top with a pair of kitchen shears, regular scissors, or a knife. If you have loss of grasp in both hands, you can operate a pair of scissors by putting a thumb or fingers from each hand in the handle holes to move the blades. WISS SHEARS are 8 inches long with a 2⅝-inch cut and have rust-resistant, nickel-plated, serrated blades. The corrugated inner handle helps release bottle tops. Cost is about $5 at houseware stores.

CHICKEN AND SHRIMP DELUXE

2 packages (6 ounces each)
   frozen chicken in white wine
   cream sauce
½ cup cooked shrimp

2 tablespoons button mushrooms,
   drained
2 tablespoons buttered bread
   crumbs

Heat chicken as directed on label. In serving dish, mix chicken, shrimp, and mushrooms. Sprinkle with crumbs. *Makes 2 servings.*

CHICKEN SUPREME

1 package (6 ounces) frozen chicken in white wine cream sauce	1 slice cooked ham toasted slivered almonds

Heat chicken as directed on label. Pour over ham slice. Garnish with almonds. *Makes 1 serving.*

EGG À LA BEEF

1 package (5¾ ounces) frozen creamed chipped beef	1 rusk or 1 slice toast 1 poached egg

Heat chipped beef as directed on label. Pour over rusk. Top with poached egg. *Makes 1 serving.*

If you have limited use or loss of function in one hand, use a pair of KITCHEN SHEARS or scissors to open plastic- and cellophane-wrapped foods. It's easier to remove the contents of sliced meat and cheese packages if you cut around all three sides and fold back the top flap. When storing cheese, slip the entire package into a plastic bag, or wrap it in plastic wrap.

A few companies distribute bacon in a sealed waxed cardboard container without an inner vacuum pack, thus eliminating one step in container opening.

WISS SHEARS

KITCHEN SHEARS

LIVER 'N BACON IN CHILI SAUCE

4 slices bacon
1 pound liver, sliced
2 tablespoons flour

1 can (10½ ounces) condensed
    onion soup
¼ cup chili sauce or catsup

Cook bacon until crisp; remove from pan, drain, and crumble. Dust liver with flour; brown in bacon drippings. Add bacon and remaining ingredients. Cover; simmer 30 minutes or until tender. Uncover and cook for a few minutes to thicken sauce. *Makes 4 servings.*

Refrigerated biscuits provide a quick topping for casseroles or a base for creamed sauces and meats. However, opening the package is sometimes a problem.

If you are working with one hand or have a weak grasp, it's best to stabilize the container while pulling off the outer wrap. Rest your less functional arm on the container and hold the can between your knees. If you are in a wheelchair, hold the container against the side of the chair.

To release the inner seal, lay the package flat on the counter and insert the KNIFE EDGE along the seam. Very light pressure will break the seal, and the container will partially open. At this point, you may bend back the container with one or both hands to expose all the biscuits. Put a sponge cloth under the end of the can to keep it from sliding.

HEARTY TUNA BISCUIT PIE

1 can (10½ ounces) condensed
    cream of mushroom soup
½ cup milk
1 teaspoon lemon juice
1 can (6½ ounces) tuna,
    drained and flaked

1 package (10 ounces) frozen
    mixed vegetables, cooked
    and drained
6 refrigerated biscuits, cut in half
1 tablespoon melted butter or
    margarine
grated Parmesan or Cheddar
    cheese

In an 8-inch-square baking dish, blend soup, milk, and lemon juice until smooth. Stir in tuna and vegetables. Bake at 450° for 10 minutes. Stir mixture. Top with border of biscuits. Brush biscuits with

KNIFE EDGE   FOLEY LID LIFTER

butter, and sprinkle with cheese. Bake 8 minutes more or until biscuits are browned. *Makes 2 to 3 servings.*

The stainless steel FOLEY LID LIFTER (No. 140) removes vacuum lids easily. The small teeth slip between the rim of the jar and its cap, and when the handles are pressed together, the teeth separate and push up the lid. If you are using one hand, or there's virtually no grasp in either hand, set the jar on a sponge cloth to keep it from sliding. Cost is about 50¢ at houseware stores.

HAMBURGERS ITALIANO

1 pound ground beef	⅛ teaspoon oregano, crushed
½ teaspoon salt	1 small clove garlic, minced, or
dash of pepper	⅛ teaspoon garlic powder
1 can or jar (2 ounces) sliced	2 tablespoons butter or margarine
mushrooms, drained	1 can (10¾ ounces) condensed
1 small onion, sliced, or ½ cup	tomato soup
frozen chopped onions	¼ cup water

Combine beef, salt, and pepper; shape into 4 patties. Brown hamburgers along with mushrooms, onion, oregano, and garlic in butter. Stir in soup and water. Cover and cook over low heat 15 minutes. Stir often. *Makes 4 servings.*

Frozen foods are easy enough to use, but closing the plastic bag to store leftovers can be difficult. This homemaker, who has the use of only one hand, keeps a STAPLER handy to do the job. She folds over the top of the bag and staples it near the edge. She reopens the bag when she needs it by simply cutting across just below the staples.

Paper clips may also be used to help prevent spilling and dehydration of bag contents.

STAPLER

CHOPS 'N BEANS ORIENTAL

6 pork chops (about 1½ pounds)
2 cans (1 pound each) barbecue beans
½ cup chopped onion (fresh or frozen) or 2 teaspoons onion powder

⅓ cup sliced celery
¼ cup sliced water chestnuts
2 teaspoons soy sauce
1 large clove garlic, minced or ⅛ teaspoon garlic powder

Brown chops. Meanwhile, combine remaining ingredients in shallow baking dish (11 x 7 x 2 inches). Press chops down into barbecue bean mixture. Bake at 375° for 45 minutes. *Makes 6 servings.*

Main Dishes—Measuring

When you are limited by lack of coordination or weakness in the hands, long-handled measuring cups are easiest to manage. When grasp is lacking, the long handle may be manipulated with both

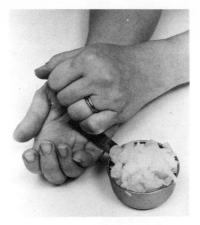

STAINLESS STEEL
MEASURING CUPS

hands. STAINLESS STEEL MEASURING CUPS come in sets of four: 1 cup, ½ cup, ⅓ cup, and ¼ cup. They are manufactured by Foley, and are available at houseware stores for about $2 per set.

BEEF BONANZA

1 pound ground beef
½ cup chopped onion (fresh or frozen) or 1 teaspoon onion powder
1 tablespoon shortening
1 can (10½ ounces) condensed cream of mushroom soup
⅓ cup water
2 tablespoons catsup

1 teaspoon Worcestershire sauce
dash of salt and pepper
1 can (8 ounces) whole white potatoes, drained and quartered
1 can (8 ounces) peas, drained, or 1 package (10 ounces) frozen peas, cooked

In skillet, brown beef and onion in shortening. Stir to break up meat particles. Add soup, water, and seasonings. Stir in vegetables. Heat slowly, stirring occasionally. *Makes 4 servings.*

The lightweight WET 'N DRY MEASURING CUP (WP40), by Westland Plastics, is actually two cups in one; it has a large handle through which the hand can be slipped for lifting when grasp is weak or lacking. The boil-proof plastic cup has easy-to-read printed gradations. Use the top for wet ingredients; then turn it over and measure the dry. Cost is about $1 at houseware stores and from mail-order firms.

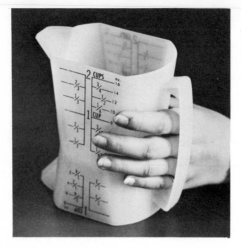

WET 'N DRY
MEASURING CUP

NOTE: Do not use this cup when extremely accurate measuring is called for, for example, as with cakes. Graduated cups that can be leveled off are best for this kind of precision.

To measure hard shortening without packing it, subtract the amount needed from the capacity of your measuring cup; fill the cup with cold water to that level, then add shortening until it reaches the top line. Thus, in a one-cup measure, ⅓ cup shortening will require ⅔ cup water. Pour out the water, and shake the shortening into a bowl or other utensil.

OVERSTUFFED CHICKEN

2 cans (10½ ounces each) condensed golden mushroom soup
⅔ cup water
1 package (8 ounces) herb-seasoned stuffing
¼ cup melted butter or margarine
2 broilers (about 2½ pounds each), split

paprika
⅓ cup chopped onion (fresh or frozen) or 1 teaspoon onion powder
generous dash of poultry seasoning
2 tablespoons butter or margarine

Combine soup with water. In roasting pan (15½ x 10½ x 2¼ inches), mix ⅔ cup soup mixture with stuffing mix and melted butter. Place broilers over stuffing; sprinkle with paprika. Cover; bake at 400° for 1 hour. Uncover, bake 30 minutes longer or until tender. Meanwhile, in a saucepan, cook onion with seasoning in butter until tender. Stir in remaining soup mixture. Heat; stir now and then. Serve with chicken and stuffing. *Makes 4 servings.*

When measuring and pouring liquids from one container to another, keep the CONTAINERS as close to each other as possible. This homemaker with cerebral palsy lines up the edge of the measuring cup with the rim of the electric skillet. She then pours the required amount of wine into the cup and tips the cup over the skillet.

CONTAINERS

BEEF BURGUNDY

1 pound sirloin cut into
  1-inch cubes
2 tablespoons butter or
  margarine
1 can (10½ ounces) condensed
  golden mushroom soup or
  beef gravy

¼ cup Burgundy or other
  dry red wine
12 small whole white onions
  (¾ pound)
2 tablespoons chopped parsley
⅛ teaspoon pepper
cooked wide noodles

In skillet, brown meat in butter. Add remaining ingredients except noodles. Cover and cook over low heat 1 hour or until tender. Stir now and then. Serve with noodles. *Makes 4 servings.*
NOTE: You may substitute 1 can (8 ounces) small whole white onions, drained, for fresh onions. Add after cooking 1 hour; heat.

When you must use only one hand or have poor coordination, it helps to place the measuring spoon or cup flat on the counter when you fill it.

Long-handled, flat-bottomed measuring spoons are more stable and easier to pick up than rounded ones.

This dishwasher-proof, four-in-one, Plastic Measuring Spoon by Ekco Housewares Company combines a tablespoon, teaspoon, half teaspoon, and quarter teaspoon in one unit. Cost is about 40¢ at department and variety stores. A similar unit is about 25¢ from the American Foundation for the Blind.

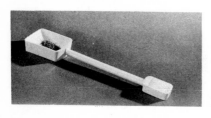

Plastic Measuring Spoon

CHICKEN STEW SCANDIA

3 slices bacon	1 teaspoon dried dill leaves
2 pounds chicken parts	1 teaspoon salt
6 small carrots, cut in ½-inch pieces	⅛ teaspoon pepper
3 medium potatoes (1 pound), quartered	1 can (8 ounces) small whole white onions, drained
2 cups water	½ cup water
	¼ cup flour

In large heavy pan, cook bacon until crisp; remove and crumble. Brown chicken in drippings. Add bacon, carrots, potatoes, 2 cups water, and seasonings. Cover; cook over low heat 45 minutes or until chicken and vegetables are tender. Stir now and then. Add onions; heat. Gradually blend ½ cup water into flour until smooth. Slowly stir into stew. Cook, stirring until thickened. *Makes 4 servings.*

Main Dishes—Cutting

A French Knife, with a 10- to 12-inch sharp blade, provides good leverage for either cutting or chopping. The point of the knife rests on the board while you rock the handle up and down, thus reducing the need for lifting and holding. Here, the homemaker with use of only one hand stabilizes the celery on the board with two stainless steel nails. (See plan for breadboard, page 202.)

SKILLET CHOPS 'N RICE

4 pork chops (about 1 pound)	1 soup can water
salt and pepper	½ cup chopped celery
1 can (10½ ounces) condensed onion soup	¼ teaspoon thyme, crushed
	½ cup raw, regular rice

Brown chops in skillet. Remove excess fat. Season with salt and pepper. Add soup, water, celery, and thyme. Cover skillet and let simmer 30 minutes. Stir in rice. Cover, and cook over low heat about 20 minutes until chops and rice are tender. *Makes 4 servings.*

You may find this Flint Swedish Cook's Knife, by Ekco, more comfortable for cutting than a standard straight knife if you have limited motion or poor coordination in your wrists and hands. The dishwasher-proof, grip-shaped handle is angled to keep your hands away from the board while cutting. The stainless vanadium blade is scalloped for surer control. Cost is about $3.50 at houseware stores.

Swedish Cook's Knife

French Knife

ORANGE-TOPPED LAMB SKILLET

4 shoulder lamb chops (about 1½ pounds)	1 medium clove garlic or ½ teaspoon garlic powder
2 tablespoons shortening	⅛ teaspoon rosemary
1 can (10½ ounces) chicken giblet or mushroom gravy	4 thick orange slices mint jelly

Brown chops in shortening. Remove excess fat. Add gravy, garlic, and rosemary. Cover and cook over low heat for 40 minutes. Stir now and then. Top each chop with orange slice. Cook 5 minutes more or until meat is tender. Garnish each orange slice with jelly. *Makes 4 servings.*

Kitchen shears or scissors are handy for trimming meats and cutting vegetables, such as green onions or asparagus, and herbs, such as fresh parsley or dill.

These Cutco Shears have slightly curved blades which make it easier to slip the tip under the object being cut. They also come apart for washing. If you have marked incoordination or overflow motions, you should probably select a pair of shears that do not come apart so easily.

Although shears are recommended for the person with moderate to good use of one or both hands, they also can be used by individuals with marked loss of grasp, as in quadriplegia or multiple sclerosis. In these cases, the homemaker can stabilize the meat or other food on a nonslip surface, such as a sponge cloth or textured carving board, and use both hands to manipulate the scissors. List price of Cutco and similar shears is about $6 at department and variety stores.

Arthritics should not use shears but should learn to utilize a large-handled knife in the most efficient ways.

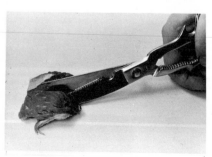

Cutco Shears

LAMB INDIENNE

1½ pounds lamb cubes (about 1½ inches in size)	½ cup water
2 tablespoons shortening	1 large clove garlic, minced
1 can (10½ ounces) condensed cream of chicken soup	1 tablespoon curry powder
½ cup sliced onion (fresh or frozen) or 2 teaspoons onion powder	dash of ground cardamom (optional)
	dash of ground coriander (optional)
	3 cups cooked rice

In a large heavy pan, brown lamb in shortening; remove excess fat. Add soup, onion, water, garlic, and seasonings. Cover and cook over low heat 1½ hours or until tender. Stir now and then. Serve with rice. If desired, offer garnishes of diced apple, chopped chutney, toasted coconut, and raisins. *Makes 4 servings.*

Main Dishes—Coating Meat

An easy, neat way to coat chicken or meat pieces is to shake them together with seasoned flour or crumbs in a PLASTIC BAG. First, measure all dry ingredients into a bag; shake to mix thoroughly. Then add chicken or meat, one or more pieces at a time, and shake well. If you are working with one hand, use a heavy-duty or quilted plastic bag so you can easily grasp the top.

PLASTIC BAG

CHICKEN ITALIANO

2 pounds chicken parts
2 tablespoons shortening
1 can (10½ ounces)
    mushroom gravy
⅓ cup chopped canned
    tomatoes

½ teaspoon oregano, crushed
¼ teaspoon salt
generous dash of pepper
2 tablespoons water
1 tablespoon flour

In a skillet, brown chicken in shortening, then remove excess fat. Add remaining ingredients except water and flour. Cover and cook over low heat 45 minutes. Stir now and then. Gradually blend water into flour until smooth; slowly stir into gravy. Cook, stirring until thickened. *Makes 4 servings.*

Main Dishes—Seasoning

You can often purchase POTTED HERBS, including basil, parsley, rosemary, chives, and others at your local grocer's. Or, if you prefer to raise your own herbs, you can buy a small greenhouse complete with pots and seeds for about $6 from mail-order houses. Home-grown herbs add a new dimension to your cooking: for delicious treats, try chopped basil over fresh tomatoes, chives with rice, or dill with cucumbers. Even if you don't grow your own fresh herbs, try the dried varieties to see how they enhance everyday meals.

ONION-ORANGE LAMB ROAST

3- to 4-pound leg of lamb
½ cup orange juice
2 tablespoons brown sugar
1 tablespoon instant minced
    onion

1 tablespoon prepared mustard
1 teaspoon rosemary, crushed
salt and pepper
1 can (10½ ounces)
    mushroom gravy

Place lamb on rack in shallow baking pan, fat-side up. Roast at 325° until done (30 to 35 minutes per pound or 175° on meat thermometer). Combine remaining ingredients except gravy; spoon over

POTTED HERBS

lamb during last 30 minutes of roasting time. Remove meat; spoon off fat. Stir gravy into drippings. Heat; stir now and then. Serve with lamb. *Makes 3 to 4 servings.*

Main Dishes—Stirring

LONG-HANDLED COOKING UTENSILS extend your reach and help keep your hands away from hot pans. They should always be used when you experience a loss of sensation in your hands. If both hands are weak, it is sometimes easier to manipulate a utensil by holding it with one hand under the handle, and the other on top for leverage.

LONG-HANDLED COOKING UTENSILS

SOUPERBURGERS

1 pound ground beef
½ cup chopped onion (fresh
  or frozen) or 2 teaspoons
  onion powder
1 tablespoon shortening

1 can (10½ ounces) condensed
  chicken gumbo soup*
1 tablespoon prepared mustard
dash of pepper
6 buns, split and toasted

In skillet, brown beef and cook onion in shortening until tender; stir to separate meat. Add soup and seasonings. Cook 5 minutes; stir now and then. Serve on buns. *Makes 6 sandwiches.*

*Or substitute tomato, vegetable, or cream of mushroom soup.

The SAFETY SPOON clips to the side of the pan so that it does not slide down into the hot pot but remains upright for easy grasping. Safety Spoons come in a set of two; one 5 inches long, the other 10 inches. The metal used is a poor heat-conductor, so that the handle does not overheat. Cost is about $1.55 per set at department stores and from mail-order firms, including American Foundation for the Blind (KC90).

VERSATILE CREAM SAUCE

1 can (10½ ounces) condensed
  cream of celery soup*

¼ to ⅓ cup milk

Pour soup into pan. Stir to blend. Add milk. Heat; stir often. *Makes about 1½ cups sauce.* Use for creaming vegetables and meats.

*Or substitute chicken or mushroom soup.

INSTANT CHEESE SAUCE

Pour 1 can Cheddar cheese soup into pan. Stir contents well to blend. Stir in ¼ to ⅓ cup milk. Heat slowly, stirring often.

4-WAY CHEESE SAUCE

Pour 1 can of any cream soup into pan. Stir to blend. Add ¼ to ½ cup milk and ½ cup shredded Cheddar cheese. Heat; stir often.

The men in your family probably look forward to gravy with meat and potatoes. You can keep them happy if you have cans of gravy

FILLED TEAKETTLE

SAFETY SPOON

(beef or chicken) or cream soup on the shelf. Also, special sauces do much to dress up a simple meal; these can easily be made with the same products.

To stabilize a pan while stirring food with one hand (or if you have poor coordination), keep a FILLED TEAKETTLE on the back burner. Move the handle of the pan around to rest against the teakettle, then stir, pushing toward the kettle.

When turning food in a skillet with a spatula, push the skillet back against the kettle.

5-MINUTE GRAVY

1 can (10½ ounces) condensed cream of celery soup*	¼ to ⅓ cup water 2 to 4 tablespoons drippings or butter

When preparing gravy for roast or fried meats, remove meat from pan and remove all but 2 to 4 tablespoons of drippings. Pour can of soup into pan; stir well to loosen browned bits. Blend in water for thickness desired. Heat; stir often. Serve with fried chicken, roast beef, roast pork, pork chops, hamburgers, or baked ham. *Makes 1½ cups gravy.*

*Or substitute chicken, mushroom, or golden mushroom soup.

SPECIAL QUICK SAUCES

Type Sauce	Use 1 Can Soup	Add and Heat
Almond for chicken, veal, or seafood	Cream of chicken or mushroom	⅓ cup water, ¼ cup chopped almonds, and 1 tablespoon minced onion (fresh or frozen) browned in butter; 1 tablespoon sherry (optional)
Curry for chicken, veal, lamb, or seafood	Cream of Asparagus, celery, or chicken	¼ to ⅓ cup milk and ¼ to 1 teaspoon curry powder
Herb for chicken, fish, veal, vegetables, or eggs	Cream of celery, chicken, or mushroom	¼ to ½ cup milk and dash of basil, marjoram, poultry seasoning, sage, or thyme

Main Dishes—Turning Food

Getting a spatula under the food in a pan to turn it or remove it is sometimes difficult, especially if you are working with one hand or weak hands, or if you are using a Teflon-coated pan.

The SKIDDER TURNER (C1430PT), by Ekco, has an angled edge which easily slides under the object being moved. It is coated with Teflon to prevent scratching and allow easy cleaning. Cost is about 80¢ at houseware stores.

GLAZED FRUITED PORK CHOPS

4 pork chops (about 1 pound)	1 can (10½ ounces) condensed
4 slices apple	beef broth or consommé
4 slices orange	1 tablespoon brown sugar
dash of ground cinnamon	2 tablespoons orange juice
dash of ground cloves	1 tablespoon cornstarch

Brown chops on both sides; remove excess fat. Place an apple and orange slice on each chop; sprinkle with cinnamon and cloves. Add soup and sugar. Cover; cook over low heat 35 minutes. Mix orange juice and cornstarch until smooth; gradually blend into soup. Cook, stirring constantly until slightly thickened. Simmer a few minutes or until chops are tender. *Makes 4 servings.*

Main Dishes—Draining

Draining vegetables or other foods in a pan is difficult when you are working with one hand or two weak hands. You may use a mesh strainer basket, as shown on page 173, or a PAN WITH A LOCK-ON LID, such as this one by Mirro Aluminum. The lid locks in place for "cook" or "drain." When turned clockwise to "drain," holes are exposed. The pan has a 2½-quart capacity and is of 10-gauge aluminum, with a black plastic handle. Cost is about $5 at houseware stores and from mail-order firms, including the American Foundation for the Blind.

SKIDDER TURNER

PAN WITH A
LOCK-ON LID

BEEF STROGANOFF

1 pound round steak, cut
    into thin strips
½ cup sliced onion or ½ cup
    frozen chopped onion
2 tablespoons butter or
    margarine

1 can (10½ ounces) condensed
    golden mushroom soup
½ teaspoon paprika
½ cup sour cream
⅓ cup water
hot buttered noodles

In skillet, brown meat and cook onion in butter until tender. Stir in soup, paprika, sour cream, and water. Cover and cook over low heat 45 minutes or until tender. Stir now and then. Serve over noodles. *Makes 4 servings.*

When your arms and hands are weak, you should select utensils with double handles to help distribute the weight of lifting. A rust-resistant, finely wired, MESH STRAINER BASKET eliminates the need to lift the pan to drain off water. It can be used for spaghetti, vegetables, boiled eggs, immersible plastic pouches, and other foods. Metal feet also allow you to use it as a steaming basket. Measurements are 7½ inches in diameter across the top, 5 inches across the bottom, and 4½ inches in depth. The handles are of metal so the strainer should be lifted with potholders. This device is about $1 from mail-order firms, variety and department stores. (Manufactured by Automatic Wire Goods Manufacturing Company, Inc.)

SPAGHETTI WITH MEAT SAUCE

½ pound ground beef
1 cup chopped onion (fresh
    or frozen)
1 teaspoon basil, crushed
1 teaspoon oregano, crushed
1 large garlic clove, minced,
    or ⅛ teaspoon garlic powder

2 cans (10¾ ounces each)
    condensed tomato soup
1 can (1 pound) tomatoes
½ pound spaghetti, cooked
    and drained
Parmesan cheese

In saucepan, brown beef. Add onion and seasonings and cook until onion is tender. Pour in soup and tomatoes. Stir to break up tomatoes. Simmer 30 minutes, stirring occasionally. Serve over spaghetti. Pass Parmesan cheese to go with it. *Makes 4 servings.*

MESH STRAINER BASKET

Main Dishes—Stove-Top Cooking

A SPLATTER SHIELD set up behind a skillet keeps walls and the back of the stove or counter clean. This lightweight aluminum shield washes easily and folds for storage. Cost is about $1 at houseware stores and from mail-order firms.

The waffled pattern of the Rubbermaid Protector Mat prevents the skillet from sliding and provides a resting place for hot pans. A 10½ by 15-inch mat is about $1; a 15½ by 17-inch mat, $1.30 at houseware stores.

Tongs may be easier and safer to use than a fork to turn meat or bacon if you are working with one hand or if coordination is lacking. The tongs illustrated are manufactured by W. R. Feemster and cost about $1 at houseware stores.

SPLATTER
SHIELD

BARBECUE BEAN SUPPER (Recipe may be doubled)

6 sausage links (about
　½ pound)
⅓ cup chopped green pepper
　(fresh or frozen)

1 can (1 pound) barbecue
　beans
2 tablespoons grated Parmesan
　cheese

Cook sausage until done. Remove all but 1 tablespoon of drippings. Add green pepper and cook until tender. Add beans and cheese. Heat, stirring occasionally. *Makes 2 to 3 servings.*

When working in a wheelchair, you often have to sit much closer to the pan in which you are cooking than the homemaker who is standing. A splatter lid will protect your face and arms from hot fat and also aids in clean-up.

Homemakers with marked lack of coordination, slowness of motions, and visual impairment will also find the splatter lid a safety aid. An aluminum FILTER-FRY COVER catches grease yet allows steam to escape freely, so foods are not steamed. It fits 9- to 11-inch-diameter pans, and costs about $1.30 at houseware and department stores, or from mail-order firms.

BEAN 'N PINEAPPLE PLATTER

4 slices bacon
2 tablespoons brown sugar
dash of ground cloves

4 pineapple slices, halved
1 can (1 pound) pork and beans
　with tomato sauce

Fry bacon until crisp; drain and crumble. Remove all but 1 teaspoon drippings. Add sugar and cloves; melt, stirring. In mixture, brown pineapple on each side. Arrange in ring on heated platter. Heat beans and bacon. Serve in center of pineapple. *Makes 4 servings.*

If weak upper extremities or arthritis make lifting difficult, you should slide pans across the counter or stove-top whenever possible. For unavoidable lifting, select pots and pans of aluminum, stainless steel, and other lightweight materials that are safe to handle and reduce stress. Look for attractive pieces that will double as serving dishes, and thereby save extra clean-up.

FILTER-FRY COVER   WEST BEND COUNTRY INN SKILLET

This WEST BEND COUNTRY INN SKILLET has a long, heat-resistant handle with a second, shorter handle to help you balance the pan if your hands are weak. It is available in gold or avocado, with an easy-to-wash black Teflon II lining. Cost is about $14 at department stores. Another brand of lightweight pans is Cerama Ware by Wear-Ever.

TOMATO-BEEF, STOVE-TOP CASSEROLE

1½ cups cubed cooked beef
1½ teaspoons onion powder
⅛ teaspoon marjoram, crushed
1 tablespoon butter or margarine
1 can (10¾ ounces) condensed tomato soup

½ cup water
2 cups cooked noodles
½ cup cut green beans, cooked
¼ teaspoon salt
2 tablespoons shredded Cheddar cheese

In saucepan, brown beef with onion powder and marjoram in butter. Add soup, water, noodles, beans, and salt. Heat; stir now and then. Garnish with cheese. *Makes 4 servings.*

Main Dishes—Basting

A baster reduces the need to lift and handle many utensils, thereby increasing kitchen safety. It has a variety of uses, including basting baked fruits and meat, separating fats from soups and gravies, adding barbecue sauce, topping or filling desserts, watering plants, and even filling a steam iron.

Glass and rubber basters work more efficiently than nylon units, but are also more prone to break. Manufacturers of both types include John L. Chaney Instrument Company, Zim Manufacturing Company, and Foley Manufacturing Company. Cost is about 70¢ to $3.

A BELLOWS-TOP BASTER is easier to use when your grasp is weak or when stress on your hands should be reduced. Push down lightly on the top surface of the bellows and then release it to draw up the liquid for transferring. The baster is of nylon and plastic and costs about 80¢ at department and variety stores.

A small can or other object under the back leg of an electric skillet allows excess oil or fat to run into one corner of the pan.

BELLOWS-TOP BASTER   FOLDED ABSORBENT PAPER TOWEL

GLORIFIED CHICKEN

2 pounds chicken parts	1 can (10¾ ounces) condensed
2 tablespoons shortening	Cheddar cheese soup*

*Or substitute cream of celery, or chicken, or mushroom soup.

In skillet, brown chicken in shortening. Remove excess fat. Stir in soup. Cover; cook over low heat 45 minutes or until tender. Stir now and then. Uncover; cook to desired consistency. *Makes 4 servings.*

Main Dishes—Skillet Meals

You can remove oil or fat from a pan with a FOLDED ABSORBENT PAPER TOWEL. Turn down the heat before you begin, and use a long fork or tongs to manipulate the paper towel. (If you are using a skillet on the range-top, first turn off the flame.)

CHICKEN BOMBAY

2 pounds chicken parts
2 tablespoons oil, butter, or margarine
1 can (10¾ ounces) condensed tomato soup
⅓ cup water

¼ cup chopped onion (fresh or frozen)
½ teaspoon garlic powder or 1 medium clove garlic, minced
1 teaspoon curry powder
¼ teaspoon thyme, crushed

In skillet, brown chicken in shortening. Remove excess fat. Add soup, water, onion, garlic, curry, and thyme. Cover. Cook over low heat 45 minutes or until tender. Stir now and then.

Serve with rice and one or more of the following: toasted slivered almonds, shredded coconut, sliced green onions, chutney, raisins. *Makes 4 servings.*

Main Dishes—Preparing Ground Meat

Meat loaf is a family favorite you probably prepare often. There are several ways to simplify preparation depending on your strength. Most homemakers have found they can mix ground meat with their hands or a fork, even if their grasp is very weak. Another method for blending meat evenly is to use a COUNTERTOP MIXER. A hand unit is not recommended for this job (with the exception of the Braun portable) since the power of portable units is not great enough and their motors will overheat. (See mixers on pages 105 to 107.)

You may either bake in a loaf pan or in a shallow pan, depending on whether it is easier for you to pack the mixture into the loaf pan or to shape loaves. If you bake the mixture in a shallow pan, it will have an attractive brown outer crust; meat loaf baked in a loaf pan does not brown all over as well.

If you shape the loaf, you may want to make two smaller ones instead of one large; the smaller units are easier to remove after baking. Transfer them to a platter, using a wide spatula like the Foley unit shown on page 188.

You may choose a metal baking pan with an enameled exterior, which is attractive enough to take right to the table for slicing and serving.

SAUCY MEAT LOAF

1½ pounds ground beef
1 can (10½ ounces) condensed cream of mushroom soup*
1 cup small bread cubes
¼ cup finely chopped onion (fresh or frozen) or 1 teaspoon onion powder

1 egg, slightly beaten
½ teaspoon salt
generous dash of pepper
¼ cup water

*Or substitute tomato or golden mushroom soup.

COUNTERTOP MIXER

Mix thoroughly beef, ½ cup soup, bread, onion, egg, salt, and pepper. Shape firmly into loaf; place in shallow baking pan (12 x 8 x 2 inches). Bake at 350° for 1 hour 15 minutes. Blend remaining soup, water, and 2 to 3 tablespoons drippings. Heat; stir now and then. Serve over loaf. *Makes 4 to 6 servings.*

Main Dishes—Making Meatballs

Meatballs of beef, lamb, veal, or pork are easy to make with one or both hands. When browned and added to prepared gravies or soups, they provide a versatile and economical meal and require no cutting at the table.

Dip your hands in a small bowl of cool water more than once; it keeps the meat from sticking during the preparation of the meatballs.

KITCHEN KING
ALUMINUM SCISSORS

If your grasp is strong in one hand, you may prefer to make meatballs with a press. This KITCHEN KING ALUMINUM SCISSORS (No. 2500) picks up the right amount of meat, forms the ball, and releases it easily. Cost is about $1.20 at houseware stores.

MANY-WAY MEATBALLS

1 pound ground beef
¼ cup fine dry bread crumbs
¼ cup chopped onion (fresh or frozen) or 1 teaspoon onion powder
1 egg, slightly beaten

¼ teaspoon salt
1 can (10½ ounces) condensed cream of celery soup*
½ cup water
2 tablespoons fresh, frozen, or dried chopped parsley

Mix beef, bread crumbs, onion, egg, and salt; shape into 16 meatballs. In skillet, brown meatballs; remove excess drippings. Stir in soup, water, and parsley. Cover and cook over low heat 20 minutes; stir often. *Makes 4 servings.*

*Or substitute 1 can condensed Cheddar cheese, golden mushroom, cream of mushroom, or tomato soup.

Main Dishes—Casseroles

Casserole recipes make one-dish meals that save energy both in preparation and clean-up. These recipes usually can be prepared in advance, on the stove or in the oven, so that the homemaker is free to prepare side dishes and do other things right before mealtime.

If weak arms and hands make lifting difficult, it's important to choose a casserole dish that's easy and safe to handle. Also, look for nonbreakable dishes, which can be used for both stove-top and oven cooking.

The CERAMA SAUCEPAN by Wear-Ever is lightweight, yet is heavy enough for long simmering and stewing. If you have a weak grasp, you can lift it by balancing the heat-resistant handles in both hands. The heat-resistant knob on the cover has a slight ridge on the top which makes it easy to manage, or it can be adapted with a dowel for hook-grasp. (See knob and handle changes under Appliances on pages 90 and 91.) The price of this 3-quart casserole (No. 38703) is about $11 at department stores. West Bend manufactures the Country Inn line which is similar. (See page 175.)

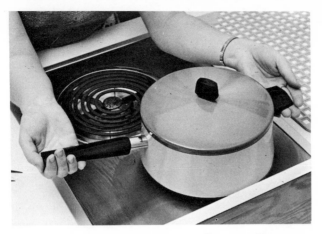

CERAMA SAUCEPAN

WESTERN-STYLE BEEF ON RICE

1½ pounds beef cubes
  (1½ inch)
2 tablespoons shortening
1 can (1 pound) tomatoes
2 medium onions, quartered
½ cup water
1 tablespoon Worcestershire
  sauce

1 teaspoon garlic powder
½ teaspoon salt
dash hot pepper sauce
⅓ cup water
3 tablespoons flour
cooked rice

In large heavy pan, brown beef in shortening; pour off fat. Add tomatoes, onions, ½ cup water, and seasonings. Cover; cook over low heat 2 hours or until meat is tender. Stir now and then. Gradually blend ⅓ cup water into flour until smooth. Slowly stir into stew. Cook, stirring until thickened. Serve over rice. *Makes 4 servings.*

Main Dishes—Oven Meals

If your reach is limited or upper extremities are weak, and your oven rack does not slide out easily, you may wish to use an oven shovel. The metal tray slips under a pan or casserole allowing you to slide it to the front of the oven rack. Then you can easily transfer

OVEN SHOVEL

it to a counter, lapboard, or wheeled table. An OVEN SHOVEL occasionally is available from mail-order firms, like Miles Kimball, or can be made at home by attaching a cookie sheet to a wooden handle.

SAVORY SHEPHERD'S PIE

1 pound ground beef
¼ cup chopped onion (fresh or frozen) or 1 teaspoon onion powder
¼ cup chopped green pepper (fresh or frozen)

1 can (10¾ ounces) condensed vegetable soup
¼ teaspoon salt
dash of thyme, if desired
seasoned mashed potatoes (about 1 cup)

Brown beef and cook onion and green pepper until tender; stir in soup, salt, and thyme. Spoon into 1-quart casserole; spoon potatoes in mounds around edge. Bake in a 425° oven 15 minutes. (In an electric skillet, prepare as above, but do not add potatoes until you are ready to serve.) *Makes 4 servings.*

Several aids are commercially available to simplify the transfer of large pieces of roasted meat or poultry from the cooking pan to the serving platter.

SLING UNIT

Here a SLING UNIT, manufactured by John Clark Brown, hoists the chicken in one easy operation. Place the stainless steel sling across the pan before adding the meat. The handles hang over the edge of the pan, or may be folded over the meat itself. With chicken, the chains serve as a handy truss to keep the wings and legs close to the body. The sling may be used with one or two hands. Cost is about $1.30 at department stores and from mail-order firms.

DELECTABLE POULTRY GRAVY

roast chicken or turkey

1 can (10½ ounces) chicken or chicken giblet gravy

Remove poultry from pan. Spoon off excess fat, saving 3 to 4 tablespoons drippings. Add gravy. Heat, stirring to loosen browned bits. Thin to desired consistency with water.

DELECTABLE MEAT GRAVY

roast beef, veal, lamb, or pork; hamburgers or steak

1 can (10½ ounces) beef or mushroom gravy

Remove meat from pan. Spoon off excess fat, saving drippings. Add gravy. Heat, stirring to loosen browned bits. Thin to desired consistency with water.

If you have the use of only one hand or your upper extremities are weak, you may find it easier to remove a baked frozen dinner from the oven if you slide a COOKIE SHEET under the dinner tray. (Never put the cookie sheet under the tray while baking, or the food will scorch on the bottom.) Be sure that the cookie sheet is completely under the tray so it will not slide off. This small cookie sheet with a raised edge is by Wear-Ever.

The potholder shown has an asbestos palm for greater protection from heat and burns. Asbestos-padded mitts are manufactured by Welmaid and cost about $2 per pair at houseware stores.

TOPPING THE FROZEN PREPARED DINNER

A simple garnish added to a frozen prepared dinner provides extra eye- and taste-appeal. Before heating, fold back foil and add garnish, then re-cover unless directed otherwise.

BEEF DINNER: Top meat with about ½ teaspoon of prepared horseradish, or a few slices of canned mushrooms and a dash of oregano.

CHOPPED BEEF SIRLOIN OR SALISBURY STEAK DINNER: Top beef with a slice of American cheese, or 1 tablespoon chopped tomato and a dash of garlic powder; or spread with 2 teaspoons of blue cheese.

FRIED CHICKEN DINNER: When you fold foil back for last 10 minutes of cooking, sprinkle chicken with about 1 tablespoon of grated Parmesan cheese; or sprinkle lightly with garlic salt.

HAM: Top sauce on ham with about 2 teaspoons of orange marmalade, or 1 tablespoon of orange juice and a bit of fresh or freeze-dried orange rind.

MEAT LOAF: Top meat with a dash of basil or oregano, or about 1 tablespoon of sliced olives; or a slice of American or Mozzarella cheese. Canned mushrooms are good too.

SWISS STEAK: Top meat with sliced olives, or grated Parmesan cheese, or a slice of Mozzarella cheese and a dash of oregano.

TURKEY DINNER: Top meat with about 1 tablespoon of toasted slivered almonds.

Frozen puff-pastry shells are a versatile and convenient way to dress up any meal. They can be stuffed with a variety of meats, vegetables, and sauces for a first-course or main dish. When filled with fruit, pudding, and/or ice cream they serve as an equally glamorous dessert. (See page 220.)

Before baking the shells, cover the COOKIE SHEET WITH FOIL. (The oil residue left by the shells is very hard to scrub off.) When the shells are done, leave them on the sheet so they will not slide as you remove the soft inner dough. Gently pry off the center top of each shell with a fork and remove the soft inner core. Then loosen the pastries from the sheet with a flat spatula.

SEAFOOD MARYLAND

1 can (10 ounces) frozen
condensed cream of shrimp
soup
½ cup light cream or milk
2 cups cut-up cooked seafood
(lobster, shrimp, fish fillets)

1 tablespoon fresh or frozen
chopped parsley
1 teaspoon lemon juice
3 or 4 baked frozen puff-pastry
patty shells

Heat soup and cream together over low heat until soup is thawed; stir often. Add seafood, parsley, and lemon juice. Heat. Serve over patty shells, rice, or toast. *Makes 3 to 4 servings.*

COOKIE SHEET   COOKIE SHEET WITH FOIL

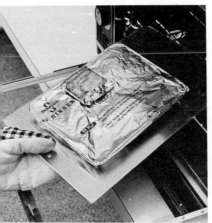

Main Dishes—Broiling

The large, heavy broiler pans found in many gas and electric ovens may be difficult for you to lift, especially if you must work from a wheelchair, or have weak arms or the use of only one hand.

You may prefer to remove food from the large broiler pan while it is hot, and leave the pan in the oven until cool to avoid spills or burns.

Or you may select a small, lightweight broiling unit such as this BROILERETTE, by Mirro Aluminum and Regal Ware. The double handles extend out far enough for a person with weak grasp to balance them on oven mitts. The drip pan may be lined with foil to reduce clean-up. Cost of the pan is about $3.50 at local houseware stores and from mail-order firms.

Persons who must function with one hand should look for a small, rectangular broiling unit that allows them to achieve a full, balanced grasp with a single hand. The Ekco broiling pan, shown on page 100 under Appliances, is lightweight and easy to manage with one hand.

To prevent steaks and chops from curling while broiling, trim fat with a sharp knife or shears. Then slash or cut meat edge every two to three inches so that it will lie flat.

HERB BROILED CHICKEN

2 packages (1 pound each) frozen chicken parts	1 teaspoon dried dill leaves, oregano, or thyme
¼ cup melted butter or margarine	1 teaspoon garlic salt generous dash of pepper

Thaw chicken as directed on package. Place chicken on broiler pan, skin-side down. Combine remaining ingredients. Brush chicken with butter mixture. Broil 8 inches from heat* for 20 minutes. Turn; brush with remaining butter mixture; broil 15 minutes more or until tender. *Makes 4 servings.*

*For gas broiler, follow manufacturer's directions.

BROILERETTE

ROAST FORKS

Main Dishes—Serving

If your arms and shoulders are weak, or you have poor coordination, try resting both elbows on the counter when lifting to provide leverage and stability.

These two, large, ROAST FORKS have a wide surface and sharp prongs to enable you to lift a roast from the pan to a serving platter. A set of two forks is about $1.70 from mail-order firms and department stores.

ZIPPY POT ROAST

3- to 4-pound beef pot roast   salt and pepper
1 can (10¾ ounces) condensed   2 to 3 tablespoons flour
  tomato soup*

In large pan, brown meat. The roast may be cooked in a high-domed electric skillet or an electric casserole, as well as on a range. Remove excess fat. Add soup and seasonings. Cover, and cook over low heat for 3 hours or until tender. Stir now and then. Remove meat from pan. Blend flour and ¼ cup water by shaking in a tightly covered container. Slowly stir into gravy. Cook; stir until thickened and smooth. *Makes 6 servings.*

*Or substitute onion soup.

Try not to overcook fish fillets, whether you are poaching, baking, or broiling them. Fish should be cooked only until it flakes easily when tested with a fork. A meat lifter or broad spatula helps remove the fish in one piece from the poaching liquid or baking pan. This FOLEY STAINLESS STEEL MEAT LIFTER costs about $1 at houseware stores.

FOLEY STAINLESS STEEL MEAT LIFTER

SAUCY FISH SKILLET FAVORITE

1 can (10¾ ounces) condensed
    Cheddar cheese soup*
¼ cup water
½ teaspoon dried dill leaves

generous dash of onion powder
1 package (1 pound) frozen
    fish fillets, thawed

In electric skillet, blend soup, water, dill, and onion powder. Add fish. Cover; cook over low heat** 10 minutes or until fish is done. Stir now and then. *Makes 4 servings.*

*Or substitute cream of celery, mushroom, or tomato soup.
**Follow manufacturer's directions.

Main Dishes—Garnishing the Canned Prepared Meal

A can opener, a little imagination, and presto, dinner is served! The variety of canned foods now available is limitless. A good stock on your pantry shelves saves many a last-minute shopping trip. Some of the most popular canned dinners include:

Beans 'n Beef in Tomato Sauce
Beans and Franks in Tomato
    Sauce
Chicken Stew
Beef Stew
Chili Con Carne (with beans)
Corned Beef Hash
Spaghetti 'n Beef in Tomato
    Sauce

Spaghetti with Meatballs; and
    with Sliced Franks
Macaroni and Cheese
Chicken à la King
Chicken 'n Gravy
Boned Chicken
Boned Turkey

There are several paperback cookbooks involving the use of canned foods which offer suggestions for stocking your larder wisely. A list of some of the most popular books appears in the bibliography. (See page 225.) Or you may write to food companies for free recipe booklets.

GARNISHES AND SERVING IDEAS

Beef Stew (19 ounces): Garnish as desired with Parmesan cheese, sour cream, sliced hard-cooked egg, French-fried onion rings. Serve over toast, biscuits, or corn bread.

Chicken Stew (19 ounces): Garnish as desired with shredded cheese, chopped olives, crisp bacon, sour cream, or sliced hard-cooked egg. Serve over toast, biscuits, waffles, or in patty shells.

Chicken 'n Gravy (15½ ounces): Cooked vegetables may be added, using about ½ cup per 1 can Chicken 'n Gravy. Try whole kernel corn, cut green beans, mixed vegetables, peas or asparagus cuts. Garnish as desired with sliced hard-cooked egg, crisp bacon bits, toasted slivered almonds, chopped chives or parsley.

Corned Beef Hash (15½ ounces): To slice hash, remove both ends of can, and push out gradually from one end using the can top as a pusher. Nails on the breadboard will stabilize the can for the homemaker using one hand. Garnish with catsup, chopped green onion, shredded cheese, mustard, or horseradish.

CHICKEN STEW WITH CURRY

¼ cup slivered almonds	1 can (1 pound, 3 ounces)
½ teaspoon curry powder	chicken stew
1 tablespoon butter or	
margarine	

In saucepan, brown almonds with curry powder in butter. Add stew. Heat; stir now and then. *Makes 2 to 3 servings.* Serve with sautéed apple rings if desired.

BRUNSWICK STEW

2 slices bacon	1 can (19 ounces) chicken stew
¼ cup chopped onion (fresh	⅓ cup cooked corn
or frozen)	

In saucepan, cook bacon until crisp; remove, cool, and then crumble. Remove all but 1 tablespoon drippings. In drippings, cook onion until tender. Add stew, corn, and bacon. Heat; stir now and then. *Makes 2 to 3 servings.*

Main Dishes—Topping

Prepared toppings for dressing up casseroles include the following items, available at most supermarkets.

Grated or sliced cheese (Parmesan and Cheddar are most common)
Flavored and unflavored bread crumbs, croutons, and prepared
    stuffing
Parsley flakes, frozen or dried
Other herbs, including dill, oregano, chives
Crisp cereals
Refrigerated biscuits
Potato chips and snack-type hand foods

When a recipe calls for finely crushed crackers, potato chips, herb stuffing, and the like, and when it is an item you cannot buy ready-prepared, then you may either whirl it in the electric blender, or use the following technique. Put the needed amount in a double plastic bag. Place the bag on the counter and crush the contents with a rolling pin, or with another FLAT, BROAD, UNBREAKABLE ITEM.

FLAT, BROAD UNBREAKABLE ITEM

PERFECT TUNA CASSEROLE

1 can (10½ ounces) condensed cream of celery soup*	2 hard-cooked eggs, sliced
¼ cup milk	1 cup cooked peas
1 can (7 ounces) tuna, drained and flaked	1 cup slightly crumbled potato chips

In 1-quart casserole, blend soup and milk; stir in tuna, eggs, and peas. Bake in a 350° oven 25 minutes. Top with chips and bake 5 minutes more, or until hot. *Makes 3 to 4 servings.*

*Or substitute chicken or mushroom soup.

Vegetables—Cleaning

Scrubbing vegetables with one hand, or with two weak or uncoordinated hands, is easier if your scrubbing brush is firmly anchored to a nonporous countertop or sink. A SUCTION-BASED BRUSH, by Anchor Brush Company, costs about $1 from self-help equipment firms including Be O/K Sales, Cleo Living Aids, G. E. Miller, J. A. Preston, and Rehab Aids. It may also be used for scrubbing flatware and dishes.

CHIPPED BEEF ON BAKED POTATOES

Use either one can of creamed chipped beef (10½ ounces) or two frozen pouches (5¾ ounces each) creamed chipped beef. Bake two potatoes; then split and fluff up contents with a fork. Pour hot creamed chipped beef over potatoes. *Makes 2 servings.*

Vegetables—Peeling

Serving vegetables and fruits in their skins is nutritious and certainly saves time and energy. However, if you wish to peel them, select a device that is comfortable for you.

SUCTION-BASED BRUSH   CALIFORNIA MIRACLE WORKER PEELER

Arthritics and people with weak grasp or poor coordination find this peeler safe and easy to use. It has a U-shaped handle to grasp or hook your fingers through for control. An oscillating blade moves smoothly over the food being peeled. This CALIFORNIA MIRACLE WORKER PEELER (Model 7-M) is manufactured by W. R. Feemster; it costs about 30¢ at houseware stores.

GERMAN POTATO SALAD

4 slices bacon	2 to 3 tablespoons vinegar
¾ cup chopped onion (fresh or frozen)	½ teaspoon sugar
	⅛ teaspoon pepper
1 can (10½ ounces) condensed cream of celery or chicken soup	4 cups sliced cooked potatoes
	¼ cup chopped parsley (fresh or frozen)
¼ cup water	

Cook bacon until crisp; remove from skillet, drain and crumble. Cook onion in bacon drippings until tender. Blend in soup, water, vinegar, sugar, and pepper. Heat; stir now and then. Add potatoes, parsley, and bacon; simmer 5 minutes. Serve hot. *Makes 6 servings.*

If you learn to handle fresh vegetables skillfully, you can save a good deal of preparation time. It's easy to acquire the basic techniques given on the next page.

BOARD WITH NAILS

Always put a paper towel on a surface before you begin peeling. When the job's done, simply pick up the towel and discard it along with the peels. If you're using a BOARD WITH NAILS to stabilize the vegetable, place your towel over the nails.

Many recipes call for small whole onions. You may use canned ones. But if you like your onions fresh, here's a simple way to peel them. First stabilize the onion on the breadboard nails, or hold it with one hand; then carefully cut through the entire outer layer of onion, from top to bottom, and peel off the outer layer with your hand. Presto! You have a quickly peeled onion! If the recipe calls for sliced onions, cut the onion in half, then lay it on its flat side to prevent it from sliding while you're slicing.

When paring a carrot, stand the vegetable on its end with two nails holding it. You can then proceed to make long swoops down the entire length of the carrot with your scraper. When you wish to cut the carrot in slices, the French-knife technique is best. Place the carrot flat on the board, and begin at the small end and work up with rocking motions of the knife.

ONIONS AMANDINE

1 can (10½ ounces) condensed cream of celery or mushroom soup

4 cups cooked, small white onions (or two 1-pound cans), drained
½ cup shredded Cheddar cheese
¼ cup chopped toasted almonds

Stir soup until smooth, mix with onions in 1½-quart casserole. Sprinkle cheese and nuts on top. Bake at 375° for 30 minutes. *Makes 6 servings.*

NOTE: If desired, substitute cashews, peanuts, or pecans for almonds.

Vegetables—Chopping

When cutting or chopping foods, keep the knife point down on the board for greater control and to conserve your energy. A large FRENCH KNIFE serves well for this purpose. (See board on page 202.)

FRENCH KNIFE

VEGETABLES AU GRATIN

2 pounds (small bunch) fresh asparagus or broccoli or small head cauliflower	1 can (10¾ ounces) condensed Cheddar cheese soup
¼ cup milk	2 tablespoons buttered bread crumbs

Wash and trim vegetables. Cook in simmering water until tender. In shallow baking dish (10 x 6 x 2 inches), arrange vegetable. Blend milk and soup; pour over asparagus. Top with crumbs. Bake at 350° for 20 minutes or until hot. *Makes 4 to 6 servings.*

Dress-Ups for Vegetables

Vegetables don't have to be the humdrum part of your menu. With additions of a few choice seasonings, they can even take the spotlight.

Since vegetables are an essential part of a balanced diet and are necessary for good nutrition, you'll want to encourage your family to eat vegetables . . . and plenty of them! The following recipes will give you some ideas for successful vegetable dress-ups.

BRUSSELS SPROUTS WITH BLUE CHEESE

1 package (10 ounces) frozen
Brussels sprouts
2 tablespoons bottled blue
cheese dressing

2 tablespoons butter or
margarine (optional)

Prepare vegetables as directed on package; drain. Stir in dressing and butter. *Makes 2 to 3 servings.*

MINTED PEAS

1 package (10 ounces)
frozen peas
1 tablespoon butter or
margarine

1 tablespoon apple-mint jelly
⅛ teaspoon mace

Prepare vegetables as directed on package; drain. Stir in remaining ingredients. *Makes 2 to 3 servings.*

Salads—Dressings

A PLASTIC STORAGE CONTAINER has a side handle for easy handling, and marked gradations for efficient measuring. Foods for refrigeration or freezing can be stored in it. It can also be put in boiling water to heat the contents. It has a covered pouring lip, and works well for shaking salad dressing and other liquid foods in small amounts. This unit holds 2 cups, and costs about 40¢. The Republic Molding Corporation makes it. Larger sizes are also available.

PLASTIC STORAGE CONTAINER

TOMATO FRENCH DRESSING

1 can (10¾ ounces) condensed tomato soup
½ cup salad oil
¼ cup vinegar
½ teaspoon dry mustard

Combine ingredients in a jar; shake well before using. (Or mix in an electric blender.) *Makes about 1½ cups dressing.* Serve with salad greens.

LOW-CAL TOMATO DRESSING

1 can (10¾ ounces) condensed tomato soup
¼ cup water
2 tablespoons lemon juice
2 teaspoons grated onion or ½ teaspoon onion powder
½ teaspoon prepared mustard
¼ teaspoon salt
generous dash of pepper

Combine all ingredients in a tightly covered container; shake until blended. Chill at least 4 hours.

Salads—Molded

Molded salads can be made directly in an attractive serving dish, eliminating the need to transfer the contents. A PLASTIC DISH comes in several bright colors, and has a plastic lid for storage. To serve, arrange salad greens around the edge of a plate, and place container in the center. Various sizes hold from 1 pint to 1½ quarts. Cost is about 35¢ and up at houseware stores.

CRANBERRY ORANGE SALAD

1 package (3 ounces) orange-flavored gelatin
½ cup boiling water

1 can (1 pound) whole-berry cranberry sauce
½ cup orange juice

Dissolve gelatin in boiling water. Stir in orange juice and cranberry sauce. Mix thoroughly. Pour into individual molds, or a single 3-cup mold. Chill until firm. *Makes 4 to 5 servings.*

To vary the salad, you may add one or more of the following:

· 1 cup diced apple
· ½ cup diced celery
· ½ cup chopped walnuts

MANDARIN ORANGE SALAD

1 can (11 ounces) Mandarin orange segments
1 package (3 ounces) orange-flavored gelatin

1 cup boiling water
½ cup cold water
2 teaspoons lemon juice

Drain fruit, reserve syrup. Dissolve gelatin in boiling water, stirring well. Add orange syrup, cold water, and lemon juice. Chill until slightly thickened. Fold in fruit. Pour into a single or 6 individual molds. Chill. *Makes 6 servings.*

Small, FLIP-OVER MOLDS are easier to handle than a single large one. They can be used to make individual salads and may be grouped together on a plate for attractive serving. To prepare molds for easy unmolding, lightly oil them. Then put them on a small tray before pouring the unjelled ingredients into the molds; this makes carrying easier and eliminates clean-up of spills. If it's hard to unmold, dip the bottom of each form individually into a bowl of warm water, and immediately invert it over the salad greens or plate.

Inexpensive copper molds in varied designs are sold by houseware stores and mail-order firms.

PLASTIC DISH

FLIP-OVER MOLDS

"V-8" ASPIC

2 envelopes unflavored gelatin   1 can (3 cups) "V-8" juice

In a saucepan, sprinkle gelatin on 1 cup cold "V-8" juice to soften. Place over low heat, stirring until gelatin is dissolved. Remove from heat; add remaining "V-8" juice. Stir, then pour into a 1-quart mold. Chill until firm. *Makes 8 servings.*

VARIATIONS:

Chill gelatin mixture until it is the consistency of unbeaten egg whites; fold in any of the following before chilling until firm:

- ¼ cup chopped celery, ¼ cup finely chopped onion, and 2 tablespoons finely chopped green pepper
- 1 cup cottage cheese and ¼ cup chopped stuffed olives
- ¼ cup chopped cucumber, 2 tablespoons minced onion, and 2 tablespoons chopped pimiento

Soups—Serving

This Farberware lightweight, stainless steel Two-Quart Teakettle (Model 756) has a heat-resistant handle which curves over the top and is set far enough away from the cover for a hand to grasp or hook the handle without hitting the hot metal. If your arm and shoulder are weak, rest your elbow on the counter while pouring.

The high knob on top may be hooked with two fingers for easy removal of the cover. Since the inside is easily accessible for cleaning, the kettle is good for heating clear soups or those with finely cut garnishes. It can also be used to cook vegetables cut in large pieces; for example, sliced carrots or cauliflower, since the water can be drained off through the spout. The spout hole is about ¾-inch wide. List price is about $9.30 at houseware stores.

Two-Quart Teakettle

HOT MULLED CONSOMMÉ

1 can (10½ ounces) condensed consommé	butter stick cinnamon, if desired
½ to 1 soup can water	

In pan, combine soup and water. Heat. Serve in cups or mugs; garnish each with a dab of butter and a stick of cinnamon. *Makes 2 to 3 servings.*

TOMATO BEEF BROTH

1 can (10½ ounces) condensed beef broth	1 can (10¾ ounces) condensed tomato soup 1½ soup cans water

In saucepan, combine all ingredients. Heat; stir now and then. *Makes 4 servings.*

When upper extremities are weak or poorly coordinated, it's safer to ladle, rather than lift and pour, hot liquids. A DOUBLE-LIPPED LADLE lets you pour from either side, and may be helpful when arm motion is limited. The handle may be built up for easier grasp with foam rubber or dowels. Double-lipped ladles cost about $1 and up at houseware stores. Manufacturers include Ekco and Foley.

SOUP COMBINATIONS

Soup makes an easy-to-prepare lunch or beginning to any meal, including breakfast. Blending two or more soups creates delicious, new taste-tempters. For dinner, add seafood or meat and serve with salad and bread or rolls. Here are some popular combinations; use cans of condensed soup and liquids as specified.

Soup Mates	*Mix These Two Soups*	*Blend with*
Country Chicken Tureen	Chicken 'n Dumplings plus Chicken Vegetable	2 soup cans water
Chuckwagon Chowder	Bean with Bacon plus Vegetable	1½ soup cans water
Hacienda Beef Soup	Vegetable Beef plus Chili Beef	2 soup cans water
Puree Mongole	Green Pea plus Tomato	1 cup milk and 1 cup water

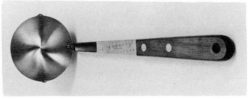

DOUBLE-LIPPED LADLE

Sandwiches—Cutting

This CUTTING BOARD is designed for the person with the use of only one hand, or poor grasp, or poor coordination in both hands.

Four rubber suction cups secure the board to the work surface. Two stainless steel nails hold vegetables and fruits while they are peeled and cut, or meat while it is trimmed and sliced. A raised corner ledge stabilizes bread or sandwiches that are being spread and cut.

The board is commercially available from Stauffer Wood Products Company for about $4.80. It may also be constructed at home, using a standard maple or hardwood cutting board. Suction cups are available at hardware stores. They cost about $1.20 per dozen from the manufacturer, Gardner Hardware. Use stainless steel nails and, if possible, have them lathed to a smooth point by a local shop. Hospital-supply firms, including Be O/K Sales, carry similar cutting boards with wood or Formica surfaces. Plans for making your own cutting board are available from the Occupational Therapy Service, Institute of Rehabilitation Medicine, New York University Medical Center, 400 East 34th Street, New York, New York 10016.

CUTTING BOARD

BASIC CHICKEN SALAD SANDWICH

1 can (5 ounces) boned chicken or turkey	1 tablespoon minced onion or ½ teaspoon onion powder
1 teaspoon lemon juice	1 tablespoon mayonnaise
½ cup chopped celery	dash of pepper

Dice chicken; mix with lemon juice. At serving time, lightly mix in remaining ingredients. Serve on crisp salad greens or use as sandwich filling. *Makes 2 to 3 servings.*

VARIATIONS:

Add 2 tablespoons chopped peanuts or toasted almonds; or ¼ to ½ teaspoon curry powder.

Sometimes a utensil originally designed for one purpose can be adapted for other uses. The PASTRY BLENDER (M1-10MP), by Ekco Housewares, has solid cutting blades that not only work for blending shortening and flour but are also good for crushing berries, fruit, or chopping hard-cooked eggs.

If you can only use one hand or have poor coordination, you may find this blender easier to use than a knife. Make sure that the bowl is deep enough to keep things from spilling over the edge, and that the container is set on a damp sponge cloth to keep it from sliding. The chrome-finished and dishwasher-proof pastry blender costs about 80¢ at houseware stores.

EGG SALAD SANDWICH

4 hard-cooked eggs, chopped	lettuce
¼ cup mayonnaise	3 hamburger buns, split
2 teaspoons prepared mustard	cooked, crumbled bacon,
½ teaspoon dried dill leaves	sliced tomato, or sweet
dash of salt	pickle slices
dash of pepper	

In bowl, combine eggs, mayonnaise, mustard, dill, salt and pepper. Arrange lettuce on buns. Top with egg salad and bacon. *Makes 3 sandwiches.*

PASTRY BLENDER

Beverages—Opening Containers

When grasp is weak or lacking, or your hands are affected by arthritis, open a Ring-Topped Can by applying simple leverage against the side of the can. Here a table knife is used. (A fork may also be employed.)

ICE CREAM FLOAT

1 cup chocolate or vanilla ice cream, or sherbet

1 can (12 ounces) ginger ale, chilled
maraschino cherries

Divide ice cream between 2 tall glasses. Pour ginger ale over ice cream. Top each glass with cherry. *Makes 2 servings.*

Ring-Topped Can

Frozen juices serve the homemaker in many ways. As beverages, they are quick and nutritious. Try blending two or more flavors for extra appeal. Orange juice and grape juice, or lemonade and fruit punch team well together.

Juices may also be used to baste meats, as for example, you may baste a ham with orange juice. Fruits gain extra sparkle when mixed with a small amount of juice. Peaches and apples stay bright when combined with orange juice, and no extra sugar is needed.

STRIP-TOP OPENING on frozen juice cans may be removed with one hand by placing the hand on top of the can and pulling the tape up. The cover releases with a slight push upward. Or you may find a bottle-cap opener helpful.

If you have loss of pinch in your hands, you may be able to catch the tab between your two fingers and release it enough to roll it around your finger for better leverage. Or you may find it easier to turn the can upside down, and open it with your can opener.

PARTY PUNCH

1 can (6 fluid ounces) frozen concentrated orange juice
1 package (10 ounces) frozen strawberries, thawed

1 tablespoon reconstituted lemon juice
1 teaspoon dried mint leaves

In pitcher, combine all ingredients. Add water as directed on juice can. Mix well. Serve in glasses. *Makes 8 servings.*

A small BOTTLE OPENER attached to the wall permits you to pry open soda bottle tops with one hand or two weak hands. This type of opener is about $1 and up at variety stores and from mail-order firms.

STRIP-TOP OPENING

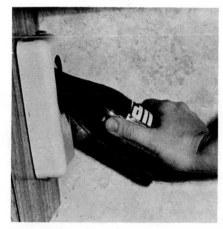

BOTTLE OPENER

CRANBERRY FIZZ

1 bottle (16 ounces) cranberry juice cocktail, chilled

1 bottle (10 ounces) citrus-flavored carbonated beverage, chilled
1 lemon, cut in 6 slices

Just before serving, mix the cranberry cocktail and carbonated beverage in a large pitcher. Or if it's easier, pour cranberry juice into 6 small glasses, and fill with carbonated citrus drink.

Cut a slit in each lemon slice from the outside to the center and hang over edge of each glass. *Makes 6 servings.*

Beverages—Handling Containers

A Lightweight Holder slips onto square paper milk containers making it easier to handle pouring when you have weak grasp or use of only one hand. This holder is manufactured by Evlo Plastics, Inc., and costs about 40¢ at variety stores.

FAVORITE WAYS WITH MILK

While milk is certainly good plain, sometimes it's enjoyable to "flavor" it up. For instance:

- Stir in a little chocolate or butterscotch syrup to taste.
- Stir into 1 glass of milk, 1 egg, 1 tablespoon honey, and vanilla to taste.
- Stir in fruit jam to taste—about 2 tablespoons per glass.

LIGHTWEIGHT HOLDER

CHOCOLATE MILK SHAKE

1 can (16 ounces) Dutch or milk chocolate pudding, chilled
3 cups milk, cold

To mix, simply stir milk into pudding until smooth or beat with an electric mixer; or you may combine ingredients in a shaker or jar with tight fitting lid; shake until smooth and frothy. *Makes 4 servings.*

Beverages—Handling Liquids

A POLYETHYLENE DECANTER has a large, single handle that helps you lift it even if you have complete loss of grasp. The spout is adjustable; it may be rotated to Open, Closed, or to a straining mesh. Measurements are marked on the sides of the base. Decanters by Republic Molding Corporation and Deka Plastics cost about 40¢ and up at variety stores.

TEENS' SPECIAL PIZZA PUNCH

1 can (24 ounces) "V-8" juice
1 small clove garlic, minced
1 small bay leaf
⅛ teaspoon oregano, crushed

In a saucepan, combine all ingredients. Heat; stir now and then. Remove garlic. Bread sticks make a nice accompaniment. *Makes 6 servings.*

POLYETHYLENE DECANTER

HOT CURRIED "V-8"

1 can (12 ounces) "V-8" juice   1 tablespoon butter
¼ teaspoon curry powder

In saucepan, heat "V-8" juice and curry; blend in butter. *Makes 3 servings.*

The BRAUN ELECTRIC JUICER (Model MPZ), by Braun Electric of America, is activated when the fruit is pressed down on the center cap. It stops when the pressure is released. If you have the use of only one hand, or weak hands, or poor coordination, you'll find this unit handy. The center post holds a larger cup for oranges as well as a small unit for lemons or limes. A built-in strainer on both units catches seeds and pulp. The base container collects large amounts of juice, and lifts out easily for pouring from either spout. All parts rinse off and have no food-catching crevices. Cost is about $30 at appliance and department stores.

TANGY TOMATO JUICE COCKTAIL

1 quart tomato juice   1 tablespoon Worcestershire sauce
¼ cup fresh or reconstituted   dash of hot pepper sauce
   lemon juice

Blend all ingredients together, and chill well. Pour into individual glasses. Garnish each glass with a mint sprig. *Makes six servings.*

Beverages—Handling Ice Trays

Removing ice from ice-cube trays can be difficult, and not everyone is fortunate enough to have an automatic ice-maker refrigerator. Filling the tray only half full is one answer to the problem. Another solution is to keep a store of ice cubes in a plastic bag, ready to dip into at a moment's notice.

This homemaker uses the MAGIC TOUCH TRAY, which has a large lever handle and a nonstick finish to make ice-cube removal easier.

Cost of these trays, made by the Inland Manufacturing Division of General Motors, is about $2 and up at houseware stores. The tray shown here makes ice slices, and costs about $4.

FAVORITE FRUIT AND VEGETABLE JUICE APPETIZERS

For unusual fruit juice drinks, try combinations like the following in half-and-half proportions:

- Apricot and orange
- Pineapple and orange
- Cranberry and apple
- Lemonade and cranberry

For colorful garnishes, try some of the following (pieces of fruit can be strung on a straw to insert in each glass):

- Mint leaves, maraschino cherry, or strawberry
- Lemon, lime, or raspberry sherbet
- Pineapple spears or melon balls
- Slice of lemon or lime

DOWN-EAST COCKTAIL

1 can (12 ounces) "V-8" juice   1½ cups clam juice

Combine juices; chill. Serve with lemon wedges. *Makes 6 servings.*

Desserts—Handling Containers

Frozen fruits and berries often come in cardboard boxes with metal ends with several types of openings. Three kinds are shown here. If you have weak hands, poor coordination, the use of only one hand, or poor vision, you'll find it easier to manage the container if you open it while the contents are still frozen, and thus avoid the need to cope with liquids.

The TAPE OPENING may be stripped off with one hand, or even with your teeth. Once the tape is removed, the top releases if you apply light pressure along the exposed edge.

The PULL-UP TOP requires strong pressure from one hand to start. If this is lacking, the tip of a table knife or fork tines may be slipped under the tab and levered against the metal edge. Then the utensil can be used to pry open the top. Again, since it is frozen, the container should be laid on its side for better control.

The PRY-UP TOP requires the use of a special flat-ended opener. Other types will not work without great difficulty. The Tap Boy, shown here, is from Vaughan Manufacturing Company, and costs about 60¢ at department and variety stores.

STRAWBERRY-PEACH BOWL

1 package (10 ounces) frozen sliced strawberries, thawed, or 1 cup fresh strawberries, halved	1 package (10 ounces) frozen peach slices, thawed whipped cream or sour cream

Mix fruits in bowl. Serve in individual dishes; top with cream. *Makes 4 servings.*

VARIATION:

Use frozen or fresh raspberries instead of strawberries. Instead of a cream topping, add 2 tablespoons of brandy, rum, or Grand Marnier to the fruit. Allow to stand at least 15 minutes.

Selecting a container with easy-to-open features is not always possible. However, here's an AEROSOL CAN with a small, important tab that releases the top quickly with the pressure of the thumb or the back of the hand. A light push on the long inner nozzle releases the contents. Even if you have almost total loss of grasp in your hands, you can manage this container without any difficulty.

TAPE OPENING   PULL-UP TOP

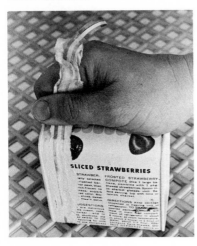 

PRY-UP TOP   AEROSOL CAN

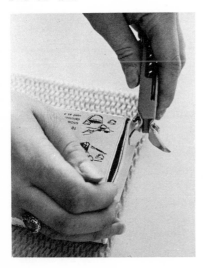 

Your grocer's shelves and frozen food compartments abound with ready-to-eat dessert ideas. There are cakes, pies, frozen turnovers and strudels, canned as well as packaged puddings, cookies, ice cream and sherbet, canned and frozen fruits, and whipped toppings.

Dressing up a dessert turns it into something extra special. Top cakes with ice cream, sherbet, or whipped toppings. Spoon fruit over pound cake. Crown fruit pies or turnovers with whipped topping, softened cream cheese, sour cream, or grated Cheddar cheese. Sprinkle puddings with chopped nuts, crushed peppermint, or coconut.

BANANA CREAM PIE

4 teaspoons cornstarch
⅓ cup water
1 can (15½ ounces) French
   vanilla pudding

1 cup sliced banana (1 large
   banana)
8-inch baked pie shell

Mix cornstarch with water; stir into pudding in saucepan. Bring to boil; cook and stir over medium heat for 3 minutes. Place alternate layers of pie filling and banana in pie shell. Chill 4 hours. If desired, garnish with whipped topping before serving.

DATE-NUT PIE

Follow Banana Cream Pie recipe, but substitute ⅓ cup chopped dates and ¼ cup chopped pecans for banana. Stir dates and nuts into filling.

If the small tab on a TEAR STRIP is difficult to start, release the end with the point of a knife to loosen it. Then press both index fingers together to catch and pull it. Once the initial tear is made, the tear strip is easy to manage.

SELF-FROSTING CAKE

1 package (2-layer) yellow
   cake mix

1 can (3½ ounces) flaked
   coconut
½ cup coarsely chopped pecans

Mix cake according to package directions. Bake as directed in oblong pan (13 x 9 x 2 inches); however, before baking, sprinkle batter with coconut and pecans.

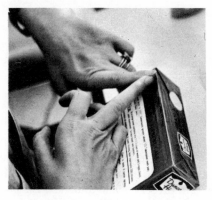

TEAR STRIP

Desserts—Opening Containers

Evaporated and condensed milk are handy products to keep on the kitchen shelves for ready use in desserts, main dishes, and beverages. However, brands without a can rim may present a problem to the person with weak hands. The easiest way to manage them is to use a regular juice-can opener to catch the slightly raised edge.

If you use canned milk frequently, a second solution is to use a PIERCING DEVICE, as shown in the diagram. Two sharp thick nails puncture the can when the bar is pressed or hit down. The second piece of wood is screwed to the top to prevent the nails from being forced up.

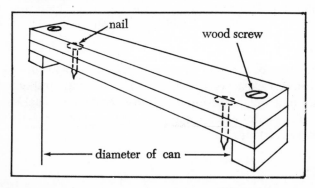

PIERCING DEVICE

Nails are hammered through second layer of wood. Top layer, held by wood screws, keeps them in place.

Use 1¼-inch-long thick nails, or a length that permits them to extend about ½ inch.

PEACH AND ALMOND MOUSSE

1 cup evaporated milk, undiluted
    generous dash of red food
    coloring (optional)
2 tablespoons lemon juice

¾ cup peach preserves
¼ cup toasted slivered almonds
12 ladyfingers, split

Freeze milk in refrigerator tray until soft ice crystals form around edges (15 to 20 minutes). Pour into mixer bowl; add food coloring, beat until just stiff (2 minutes). Add lemon juice; whip until very stiff (2 minutes longer). Fold in preserves and almonds. Line 8-inch-square baking pan with 6 split ladyfingers; pour in milk mixture. Top with remaining ladyfingers. Freeze 3 hours or overnight. *Makes 8 servings.*

Desserts—Separating Eggs

When whites must be separated from the yolks, you may use a commercially available egg separator or a FUNNEL. The white falls to the bottom of the container while the yolk remains in the separator or funnel.

SNOW PEAK PUDDING

1 can (15¾ ounces) rice
    pudding
¼ cup raisins

2 egg whites
4 tablespoons sugar

Spoon pudding into four individual baking dishes or soufflé cups. Stir a few raisins into each portion. Beat egg white until frothy. Add sugar. Beat until stiff peaks form. Spread over pudding. Bake at 400° for 8 to 10 minutes or until the meringue is golden brown. Serve warm. *Makes 4 servings.*

Desserts—Mixing

Lightweight, stainless steel bowls are usually the easiest to use when mixing a cake or other batter. Look for a set of bowls with flat bottoms; these can be set securely on a counter or sponge cloth without tipping. Some bowls have single rings. These are particularly useful if you are working with only one hand, or have a weak grasp—they help you in lifting the bowl to empty its contents. STAINLESS STEEL BOWLS manufactured by Ekco, Farberware, and others cost about $5 to $10 per set of 3 at houseware and department stores.

If your upper extremities are weak or poorly coordinated, it may be easier to hold a bowl in your lap while mixing. The edge of the electric mixer rests on the side of a deep, stainless steel bowl while you add ingredients. This homemaker on a high kitchen chair uses a damp sponge cloth between the bowl and the counter edge to provide enough friction to keep the bowl from turning.

FUNNEL   STAINLESS STEEL BOWLS

MIDNIGHT BAVARIAN CREAM

2 envelopes unflavored gelatin
½ teaspoon cinnamon
1 cup cold water

2 cans (1 pound each) Dutch
  or milk chocolate pudding
4 egg whites
whipped cream and cinnamon

This requires an 8-cup mold (or use half of the recipe and put it in a 4-cup mold). Prepare mold by lightly oiling the insides for easy unmolding. In saucepan, sprinkle gelatin and cinnamon over water; stir over low heat until dissolved. Gradually blend gelatin into pudding; chill until slightly thickened. Beat egg whites until soft peaks form; then fold in pudding mixture. Pour into mold. Chill about 4 hours or overnight. Garnish with whipped cream and cinnamon as desired. *Makes 8 servings.*

When you have moderate weakness in your arms, it may be easier for you to place a BOWL in the bottom of the sink while mixing. This helps keep your shoulder and arm at a more relaxed angle. The bowl may be stabilized by resting it on a damp sponge cloth.

FROZEN FUDGE CUPS

1 can (1 pound) Dutch or
  milk chocolate pudding
⅓ cup milk
⅓ cup miniature marshmallows

maraschino cherries
7 paper cups (3-ounce size)
7 wooden sticks

Combine all ingredients except cherries. Place a cherry in each cup. Fill cups with pudding mixture. Insert sticks. Freeze until firm, about 5 hours or overnight. Take from freezer and let stand a few minutes before removing paper to serve. *Makes 7 servings.*

The MIXSTIR, by Wear-Ever, is a handy utensil for stirring sauces, puddings, batters, and liquids, as well as for scrambling eggs, and blending dry ingredients. The coil reaches into the corners of the pan, and keeps the bottom clean with slight stirring motions, while the contoured grip is comfortable to hold. Persons with poor coordination or weak upper extremities have found this kitchen tool versatile. Cost is about $2 at department stores.

BOWL   MIXSTIR

A wire whisk also works well for mixing up quick batters, eggs, and blending gravies or soups. The thin wires have less density than a spoon or heavier unit and thus require less power to wield, especially when your upper extremities are weak or tire easily. Whisks come in various sizes with small coiled wire or large wooden handles. If you have a moderately involved grasp, you'll probably prefer a larger handle; if you have almost complete loss of grasp, as in quadriplegia, you'll find that a small coiled handle slips into the palmar pocket of a Universal Cuff. (See page 124.) Wire whisks cost from 50¢ up to $2 at houseware and culinary specialty stores.

EASY POT DE CRÈME

1 can (1 pound) Dutch chocolate pudding	½ cup heavy cream, whipped crumbled macaroons
1 tablespoon brandy	

Fold pudding and brandy into cream until smooth. Pour into individual serving dishes. Chill. Garnish with macaroons. *Makes 4 to 6 servings.*

This West Bend Grip 'n Whip stainless steel, 3-quart MIXING BOWL has a pouring lip, graduation marks for measuring, and a large handle that's easy to lift with one hand. The handle is wide enough to pick it up with a hook-grasp by slipping the entire hand inside the handle. The base is flat for good stability on a counter or sponge cloth, and the sides are deep enough to prevent splattering. It can also be used on the stove. Grip 'n Whip costs about $3.50 at houseware stores.

MIXING BOWL

The cupcake pan, by Wear-Ever, is Teflon-lined for easier removal of cupcakes and faster washing. A sponge cloth prevents the pan from sliding.

FANCY TOUCHES FOR CUPCAKES

When you bake cake, it's often simpler to use cupcake pans, since these can be baked in the paper liners, saving clean-up. Cupcakes are easy to frost; simply dip and twirl the top of each cake in prepared frosting. (Also, you don't have to bother to slice the cake when you serve it.)

Decorations for White Frosted Cakes:

• Colored sugar crystals—dip frosted cake in crystals.
• Silver shot—dip frosted cake in silver shot.
• For Christmas—sprinkle red sugar crystals in the center,
  green around the outside edge of frosting. Or sprinkle
  green sugar crystals over all and dot with red-hot cinnamon candies.

Decorations for Chocolate Frosted Cakes:

• Dip top of frosted cake in chopped toasted nuts.
• Top with one or two halves of maraschino cherries.
• Place a few miniature marshmallows on each cake.

Desserts—Baking

Turning a cake pan over to release the cake usually requires dexterity and the use of both your hands. A LAYER CAKE PAN with a removable bottom, like this one made by Wear-Ever Aluminum (No. 2725), makes the job easier. Loosen the cake around the edges, flip the entire cake over with one hand onto a plate or rack, and then press gently on the bottom to release the outer ring. Once the ring is removed, slip a flat metal spatula between the pan bottom and the cake to release the bottom.

When frosting a cake, simply turn the first half onto the serving plate, remove the pan, and frost the bottom layer; next place the second half on top with the pan bottom still attached. Now release the bottom, which has provided enough rigidity to enable you to move the layer easily.

LAYER CAKE PANS

QUICK TOMATO SPICE CAKE

1 package (2-layer) spice cake mix	1 can (10¾ ounces) condensed tomato soup
½ cup water	2 eggs

Mix *only* the above ingredients, following directions on the package of cake mix. If desired, fold in 1 cup chopped walnuts. Bake as directed. Frost with Cream Cheese Frosting or other favorite white frosting.

CREAM CHEESE FROSTING

Blend 2 packages (3 ounces each) cream cheese (softened) with 1 tablespoon milk. Gradually add 1 package (1 pound) sifted confectioners' sugar (about 5 cups); blend well. Mix in ½ teaspoon vanilla extract (optional). Makes enough frosting for two 8-inch layers. If desired, sprinkle top with maple sugar.

Desserts—Pastry Shells

Ready-to-bake, FROZEN PASTRY SHELLS serve as a base for elegant, easy-to-prepare desserts. They may be filled with prepared puddings, fruit combinations, or ice cream. Toppings include fruit, chocolate and other sauces, whipped cream, chopped nuts or glacé fruits.

FROZEN
PASTRY SHELLS

APRICOT CRÈME TARTS

1 can (8¾ ounces) apricot
  halves, drained
1 package frozen pastry shells

1 can (15½ ounces) French
  vanilla pudding

Bake pastry shells according to directions. Remove centers and let cool. Place one apricot half in the bottom of each pastry shell. Fill with pudding and top with remaining apricots. Garnish with almonds and whipped topping if desired. *Makes 6 servings.*

Desserts—Pies

Regular pastry and graham cracker READY-PREPARED CRUSTS are available at the frozen food and prepared mix sections of your supermarket. Graham cracker crusts provide a perfect base for frozen and non-frozen cream pies. Ready-prepared puddings and desserts make quick fillings. Follow directions on the can or box to make a firm enough filling. Extra flavorings and toppings may be added as desired.

If you want to add a special touch, sprinkle the bottom with grated coconut, ground almonds, or chopped nuts just before baking. Then add your favorite filling.

READY-PREPARED CRUSTS

:SE PIE

:es) French	¼ cup pineapple syrup
	1 envelope unflavored gelatin
μαςκages (3 ounces each)	½ cup cold water
cream cheese, softened	9-inch baked graham cracker
½ cup crushed pineapple,	crust
drained	

In a large bowl, gradually blend the pudding into the cheese. Stir in pineapple and syrup. In saucepan, sprinkle gelatin over water to soften; stir over low heat until dissolved. Gradually stir gelatin into pudding mixture. Pour into pie shell. Chill. *Makes one 9-inch pie.*

When you wish to roll out your own pie crust, use waxed paper on both sides of the dough, or a plastic pie-crust maker, to ease the transfer of dough to the pan and lessen clean-up. Slightly moisten the counter underneath the waxed paper or plastic to prevent sliding.

A ZIPPERED PIE-CRUST MAKER, by Ropa-Maid, makes the perfect size crust for a 9-inch pan, and is especially helpful when you are working with one hand or have poor coordination. A loop slipped through the zipper tab makes it easier to handle when pinch is weak or lacking. Price is about $1 from mail-order firms, including Hanover House.

If you have the use of only one hand, you don't need a special

ZIPPERED PIE-CRUST MAKER

ADDING WATER

rolling pin; you can use a regular one by guiding it with your single hand resting on the center of the pin.

LEMON CREAM PIE

1 can (15 ounces) sweetened condensed milk	1 teaspoon lemon rind
	8-inch baked pie shell, cooled
2 eggs, separated	¼ teaspoon cream of tartar
½ cup lemon juice	¼ cup sugar

In bowl, blend milk, egg yolks, lemon juice, and lemon rind; pour into crust. In small bowl, beat whites with cream of tartar until soft peaks form. Gradually add sugar, beating until stiff peaks form. Spread meringue over filling, sealing to edge of crust. Bake at 325° for 12 to 15 minutes or until meringue is golden brown. *Makes one 8-inch pie.*

Desserts—Oven

Lifting and carrying can be a problem because of weak upper extremities or poor coordination, ADDING WATER to a pan *after* it's on the stove or in the oven is safer and more convenient.

BAKED APPLES

Allow 1 apple per serving. For each apple, use:

⅛ teaspoon cinnamon	1 tablespoon white or brown sugar

Wash and core, but do not peel apples. Place apples in oven casserole dish. Sprinkle cinnamon and sugar over top. Add water to depth of ¼ inch in pan. Bake about 45 minutes in a moderate oven, 350°.

NOTE: Extra apples may be baked and frozen. Canned, sliced, unsweetened apples may also be baked. Sprinkle with cinnamon and sugar. Bake about 25 minutes in moderate oven, 350°.

Desserts—Quick Ideas

Combining two or more prepared convenience foods can result in easy and elegant desserts.

REFRIGERATED ROLLS make flaky or spicy tops for fruit cobblers. Here cinnamon rolls top a cobbler made of cherry and apple pie fillings. Other canned fruit pie fillings include peach and blueberry. Or you may make your own favorite fruit fillings, substituting the biscuits for a pie crust. (Hints for opening refrigerated biscuits are given on page 156.)

REFRIGERATED ROLLS

JIFFY CHERRY-APPLE PIE

1 jar or can (1 pound 8 ounces) apple pie filling
1 jar or can (1 pound 8 ounces) cherry pie filling

1 teaspoon grated orange rind (optional)
8 refrigerated biscuits

In shallow baking dish (10 x 6 x 2 inches), combine pie fillings and rind. Bake at 425° for 20 minutes or until hot. Stir. Top with biscuits. Bake 15 minutes more or until biscuits are done. *Makes 8 servings.*

NOTE: If desired, before baking with biscuits, brush the tops of the biscuits with butter and sprinkle them with cinnamon.

HELPFUL COOKBOOKS AND MEAL PLANNING REFERENCES

THE COMPLETE ELECTRIC SKILLET-FRYPAN COOKBOOK. Roberta Ames. The New American Library, Inc., New York, 1969. 95¢.

A COOKBOOK FOR THE LEISURE YEARS. Phyllis MacDonald. Doubleday & Company, Inc., Garden City, New York, 1967. $4.50.

COOKING FROM THE PANTRY SHELF. Myra Waldo. Collier Books, New York, 1962. 95¢.

COOKING WITH ELECTRIC APPLIANCES. Poppy Cannon. MacFadden-Bartell Corp., New York, 1968. 75¢.

FOOD AND ARTHRITIS. Gaynor Maddox. Taplinger Publishing Co., Inc., New York, 1969. $6.50.

HELOISE'S KITCHEN HINTS. Heloise. Pocket Books, a division of Simon & Schuster, Inc., New York, 1963. 75¢.

I HATE TO COOK BOOK. Peg Bracken. Fawcett Publications, Greenwich, Connecticut, 1965. 60¢.

THE SPECIAL DIET COOK BOOK. Marvin Small. Hawthorn Books, Inc., New York, 1969. $5.95.

If you have favorite convenience foods, and want other recipes for using them, write directly to the company.

BASIC INFORMATION ON HOMEMAKING AND EQUIPMENT TO HELP YOU BE INDEPENDENT. Some of these books may be carried by your local library.

AIDS TO INDEPENDENT LIVING: SELF-HELP FOR THE HANDICAPPED. Edward W. Lowman and Judith L. Klinger. McGraw-Hill Book Company, New York, 1969. $39.00.

THE ARMCHAIR SHOPPER'S GUIDE. Delphine C. Lyons. Essandess Special Editions, a division of Simon & Schuster, Inc., New York, 1968. $1.50.

CONSUMERS ALL—THE YEARBOOK OF AGRICULTURE. U. S. Department of Agriculture, Superintendent of Documents, Washington, D. C., 1965. $2.75.

HOMEMAKING FOR THE HANDICAPPED. Elizabeth E. May, Neva R. Waggoner, and Eleanor M. Boettke. Dodd Mead Co., New York, 1966. $7.50.

A Manual for Training the Disabled Homemaker (Rehabilitation Monograph VIII). Howard A. Rusk, *et al*. The Institute of Rehabilitation Medicine, New York University Medical Center, New York, 1967. $2.

You on Crutches, How To Help Them Help You. Nora Works. Carlton Press, New York, 1968. $2.50.

Publications on general meal planning and nutrition information are also available from the Superintendent of Documents, Washington, D.C. 20025. Write for a list.

PERIODICALS

The following publications also offer special articles of interest to you.

Accent on Living
802 Reinthaler, Bloomington, Illinois 61701. $2 per year, quarterly.

Toomey J. Gazette
Box 149, Chagrin Falls, Ohio 44022. Practical publication on personal experiences by severely disabled individuals. Articles include homemaking, housing, education, employment. Free to severely disabled. Donations asked from non-disabled.

ORGANIZATIONS AND AGENCIES OFFERING INFORMATION AND HELP

There are many organizations set up to answer questions you may have about your disability, to distribute information, and to help you solve problems. In many instances local chapters can offer you more personal help than the national headquarters.

American Association of
 Retired Persons
1225 Connecticut Avenue, N.W.
Washington, D.C. 20036

American Cancer Society,
 Incorporated
National Office
219 East 42nd Street
New York, New York 10017

American Diabetes
 Association, Inc.
18 East 48th Street
New York, New York 10017
ADA Forecast

American Dietetic Association
620 North Michigan Avenue
Chicago, Illinois 60611
Information on special diets.

AMERICAN FOUNDATION FOR
THE BLIND
15 West 16th Street
New York, New York 10011

AMERICAN HEART ASSOCIATION
44 East 23rd Street
New York, New York 10010

AMERICAN HOME ECONOMICS
ASSOCIATION
1600 20th Street, N.W.
Washington, D.C. 20009

AMERICAN OCCUPATIONAL
THERAPY ASSOCIATION
251 Park Avenue South
New York, New York 10010

AMERICAN PHYSICAL
THERAPY ASSOCIATION
1740 Broadway
New York, New York 10019

THE ARTHRITIS FOUNDATION
1212 Avenue of the Americas
New York, New York 10036
Home Care Booklet

CANADIAN ARTHRITIS AND
RHEUMATISM SOCIETY
National Office
900 Yonge Street
Toronto 5, Ontario, Canada

HOME ECONOMICS
EXTENSION DIVISION
U. S. Department of Agriculture
Washington, D.C. 20210

INSTITUTE OF REHABILITATION
MEDICINE
New York University
Medical Center
400 East 34th Street
New York, New York 10016

MUSCULAR DYSTROPHY
ASSOCIATIONS OF AMERICA, INC.
1790 Broadway
New York, New York 10019

NATIONAL COUNCIL ON
THE AGING
315 Park Avenue South
New York, New York 10010

NATIONAL COUNCIL OF
SENIOR CITIZENS
(National Senior Citizens Education Research Center, Inc.)
1627 K Street, N.W.
Washington, D.C. 20006

THE NATIONAL FOUNDATION
—MARCH OF DIMES
800 Second Avenue
New York, New York 10017

NATIONAL LEAGUE FOR NURSING
10 Columbus Circle
New York, New York 10019

NATIONAL MULTIPLE
SCLEROSIS SOCIETY
257 Park Avenue South
New York, New York 10010

NATIONAL PARAPLEGIA
FOUNDATION
333 North Michigan Avenue
Chicago, Illinois 60601

NATIONAL SOCIETY FOR CRIPPLED
CHILDREN AND ADULTS
2023 West Ogden Avenue
Chicago, Illinois 60612

NATIONAL TUBERCULOSIS
ASSOCIATION
American Review of Respiratory
Diseases
1740 Broadway
New York, New York 10019

UNITED CEREBRAL PALSY
  ASSOCIATIONS, INC.
321 West 44th Street
New York, New York 10036

U. S. SOCIAL SECURITY
  ADMINISTRATION
Division of Disability Operations
6401 Security Boulevard
Baltimore, Maryland 21235

VISITING NURSE ASSOCIATION
(check local address)

VOCATIONAL GUIDANCE AND
  REHABILITATION SERVICES
2239 East 55th Street
Cleveland, Ohio 44103
*Clothing for handicapped women.
  Catalog.*

HELPFUL SOURCES

When purchasing any of the items shown in this book, we recommend that you check your telephone book first, and then try your local department, houseware, stationery, and specialty stores. If a specific store does not have the item you desire, they will often order it from their jobber. If this is not successful, you may write the manufacturer, who in most cases will take personal orders, or will refer your order to a local source.

ADDRESSES AND SOURCES FOR KITCHEN EQUIPMENT AND TOOLS

ALKCO MANUFACTURING COMPANY
4224 North Lincoln Avenue
Chicago, Illinois 60618

ALUMINUM HOUSEWARES, INC.
411 North 7th Street
St. Louis, Missouri 63101

AMERICAN LA FRANCE
225 Delaware Avenue
Elmira, New York 14902

AMERICAN SPONGE AND
CHAMOIS COMPANY, INC.
47-00 34th Street
Long Island City, New York 11101

AMERICAN STANDARD
Plumbing and Heating Division
40 West 40th Street
New York, New York 10018

AMERICAN STANDARD PRODUCTS
1201 Dupont Street
Toronto 4, Ontario, Canada

ANCHOR BRUSH COMPANY
625 South Railroad Avenue
Montgomery, Illinois 60538

AUTOMATIC WIRE GOODS
MANUFACTURING COMPANY, INC.
385 Gerard Avenue
New York, New York 10051

BANCROFT'S
251 East Fifth Street
St. Paul, Minnesota 55101
(General mail-order firm)

BANDWAGON, INC.
401 Summer Street
Boston, Massachusetts 02210

BAUSCH & LOMB SAFETY PRODUCTS
655 St. Paul Street
Rochester, New York 14605

BAZAR FRANÇAIS
666 Sixth Avenue
New York, New York 10010
(Culinary specialties)

L. L. BEAN, INC.
248 Main Street
Freeport, Maine 04032

229

BE O/K SALES COMPANY
Box 32
Brookfield, Illinois 60513

BEREA COLLEGE
Student Industries
Berea, Kentucky 40403

BIO-TEX DEVICES, INC.
527 Atlantic Avenue
Freeport, New York 11520

BLACK ANGUS, INC.
41 Meadow Street
Winsted, Connecticut 06098

BRAUN ELECTRIC OF AMERICA, INC.
151 Michigan Street
Toledo, Ohio 43624

BRECK'S OF BOSTON
401 Summer Street
Boston, Massachusetts 02210
(General mail-order firm)

E. F. BREWER
P.O. Box 711
Butler, Wisconsin 53007

JOHN CLARK BROWN
1 Montgomery Street
Belleville, New Jersey 07109

CASUAL LIVING
Route 6, Stony Hill
Bethel, Connecticut 06801

CENTRAL MANUFACTURING
    COMPANY, INC.
9400 Valley View
Macedonia, Ohio 44056

CHANEY INSTRUMENT CO.,
    see under JOHN L. CHANEY

CHICAGO METALLIC
    MANUFACTURING COMPANY
200 South Ela Street
Lake Zurich, Illinois 60047

CLEO LIVING AIDS
3957 Mayfield Road
Cleveland, Ohio 44121

COOK COMPANY, *see under*
    JOAN COOK COMPANY

CORNING GLASS WORKS
Centerway
Corning, New York 14830

CUISINIÈRE, *see under*
    LA CUISINIÈRE, INC.

CUTCO CUTLERY
Division of Wear-Ever
    Aluminum, Inc.
205 East 42nd Street
New York, New York 10036

J. P. DARBY, INC.
New Hyde Park, New York 11040
(General mail-order firm)

DAZEY PRODUCTS COMPANY
Seal-A-Meal Division
4500 East 75 Terrace
Kansas City, Missouri 64132

DEKA PLASTICS, INC.
906 Westfield Avenue
Elizabeth, New Jersey 07206

DELTA FAUCET COMPANY
Division of Masco Corporation
Route #4
Greensburg, Indiana 47240

DENNIS MITCHELL INDUSTRIES
4424 Paul Street
Philadelphia, Pennsylvania 19124

DOMINION ELECTRIC CORPORATION
120 Elm Street
Mansfield, Ohio 44900

DOWNS AND COMPANY
1014 Davis Street
Evanston, Illinois 60204
(General mail-order firm)

DRAKE, *see under*
WALTER DRAKE AND SONS

E. I. DUPONT DE NEMOURS AND
COMPANY, INC.
350 Fifth Avenue
New York, New York 10001

EASY DAY
MANUFACTURING COMPANY
P.O. Box 747
9-21 Station Street
Boston, Massachusetts 02147

EDLUND MANUFACTURING
COMPANY, INC.
Home Avenue
Burlington, Vermont 05401

E. F. BREWER, *see under* BREWER

EKCO HOUSEWARES COMPANY
9234 West Belmont Avenue
Franklin Park, Illinois 60131

ELJER PLUMBINGWARE
Division Wallace-Murray Corporation
2 Pennsylvania Plaza
New York, New York 10001

ELKAY MANUFACTURING COMPANY
2700 South 17th Avenue
Broadview, Illinois 60155

EMPIRE BRUSHES
200 William Street
Port Chester, New York 10574

EVEREDY COMPANY
8 East Street
Frederick, Maryland 21701

EVEREST AND JENNINGS
1803 Pontius Avenue
Los Angeles, California 90025

EVLO PLASTICS, INC.
1432 Tiffin Street
Sandusky, Ohio 44870

FARBERWARE
S. W. Farber
Division of Walter Kidde and
Company, Inc.
415 Bruckner Boulevard
Bronx, New York 10454

"FASHION-ABLE"
P.O. Box 23188
Fort Lauderdale, Florida 33307
(Clothes, especially undergarments
for handicapped women)

FEDTRO, INC.
Federal Electronics Sales Division
Federal Electronics Building
Rockville Centre, New York 11571

W. R. FEEMSTER
131 North Main Street
Brooklyn, Michigan 49230

FLEX-STRAW
1504 10th Street
Santa Monica, California 90400

FOLEY MANUFACTURING COMPANY
33 North East 5th Street
Minneapolis, Minnesota 55413

FRIGIDAIRE SALES CORPORATION
500 East Hunting Park Avenue
Philadelphia, Pennsylvania 19124

GARDNER HARDWARE COMPANY
515 Washington Avenue North
Minneapolis, Minnesota 55406

GAYDELL, INC.
3030 Wilshire Boulevard
Santa Monica, California 90403

G. E. MILLER, INC.,
see under MILLER

GEM ELECTRIC MANUFACTURING
COMPANY, INC.
Hauppauge, New York 11787

GENERAL CABLE CORPORATION
(Cornish Wire Company)
730 Third Avenue
New York, New York 10017

GENERAL ELECTRIC CO.
Appliance Park
Louisville, Kentucky 40225
(Large appliances)

GENERAL ELECTRIC CO.
Housewares Division
2185 Boston Avenue
Bridgeport, Connecticut 06602
(Small appliances)

GENERAL ELECTRIC CO.
Wiring Device Department
95 Hathaway Street
Providence, Rhode Island 02907

GENERAL SLICING MACHINES
COMPANY, INC.
Walden, New York 12586

GIBRALTAR INDUSTRIES, INC.
645 Michigan Avenue
Chicago, Illinois 60611

GIFTS AND GADGETS OF DALLAS
724 South Sherman Street
Richardson, Texas 75080
(General mail-order firm)

GRACIOUS LIVING
Berkeley, Rhode Island 02864
(General mail-order firm)

GRAYLINE HOUSEWARES, INC.
1616 Berkley Street
Elgin, Illinois 60120

HAMILTON BEACH CO.
Scovill Division
99 Mill Street
Waterbury, Connecticut 06720

HAMILTON COSCO, INC.
State Street
Columbus, Ohio 47201

HAMMACHER SCHLEMMER
145 East 57th Street
New York, New York 10022
(Mail-order catalog)

HANOVER HOUSE
Hanover, Pennsylvania 17331
(General mail-order firm)

W. R. HAUSMANN WOODWORK, INC.
1545 Inwood Avenue
New York, New York 10052

HI-JAC CORPORATION
Chattanooga, Tennessee 37409

S. A. HIRSH
MANUFACTURING COMPANY
8051 Central Park Avenue
Skokie, Illinois 60076

THE HOBART
MANUFACTURING COMPANY
Kitchen Aid
World Headquarters Avenue
Troy, Ohio 45373

HYDE TOOLS
54 East Ford Road
Southridge, Massachusetts 01550

INLAND MANUFACTURING DIVISION
General Motors Corporation
2727 Inland Street
Dayton, Ohio 45406

INTERNATIONAL PAPER COMPANY
Long-Bell Division, Box 579
Longview, Washington 98632

INVALEX COMPANY
741 West 17th Street
Long Beach, California 90813

J. A. PRESTON CORPORATION,
  see under PRESTON

JOAN COOK COMPANY
1241 N.E. 8th Avenue
Fort Lauderdale, Florida 33304
(General mail-order firm)

JOHN OSTER MANUFACTURING
  COMPANY, *see under* OSTER

JOHNNY APPLESEED'S
Box 615
Beverly, Massachusetts 01915

JOHN CLARK BROWN,
  see under BROWN

JOHN L. CHANEY
  INSTRUMENT COMPANY
220 Broad Street
Lake Geneva, Wisconsin 53147

J. WISS & SONS COMPANY,
  see under WISS

KENDALL
2714 Holly Avenue
Arcadia, California 91006

KERR WIRE PRODUCTS COMPANY
933 North Cicero Street
Chicago, Illinois 60651

KIMBALL, *see under*
  MILES KIMBALL

KITCHEN KING
Bethpage Sweet Hollow Road
Bethpage, New York 11714

KNAPE AND VOGT
  MANUFACTURING COMPANY
658 Richmond Street
Grand Rapids, Michigan 59402

THE KREBS
Dunn's Corners
Westerly, Rhode Island 02891

LA CUISINIÈRE, INC.
903 Madison Avenue
New York, New York 10021

LAMSON AND GOODNOW
  MANUFACTURING COMPANY
Shelburne Falls,
Massachusetts 01370

G. S. LEINER & COMPANY
2564 Park Avenue
New York, New York 10051

L. L. BEAN, INC., *see under* BEAN

LUMEX, INC.
100 Spence Street
Bay Shore, New York 11706

LUX CLOCK
  MANUFACTURING COMPANY
Robert Shaw Controls
95 Johnson Street
Waterbury, Connecticut 06710

LYNCO
28880 Southfield Road
P.O. Box 34
Lathrup Village, Michigan 48037

MAISON MICHEL
Michel Building
New Hyde Park, New York 11040
(Culinary specialties and
  cooking aids)

MASONITE CORPORATION
29 North Wacker Drive
Chicago, Illinois 60606

MILES KIMBALL
41 West Eighth Avenue
Kimball Building
Oshkosh, Wisconsin 54901
(General mail-order firm)

G. E. MILLER, INC.
484 South Broadway
Yonkers, New York 10705

MINNESOTA MINING AND
    MANUFACTURING COMPANY
2501 Hudson Place
St. Paul, Minnesota 55119

MIRRO ALUMINUM
Manitowoc, Wisconsin 54220

MONTGOMERY WARD
Albany, New York 12201

NASCO-HERRSCHNER
Fort Atkinson, Wisconsin 53538

NATIONAL BRUSH COMPANY
101 Illinois Avenue
Aurora, Illinois 60507

NATIONAL PRESTO INDUSTRIES, INC.
1515 Ball Street
Eau Claire, Wisconsin 54702

NESCO DIVISION
The Hoover Company
St. Louis, Missouri 63116

NEVCO
500 Nephrin Avenue
Yonkers, New York 10700

N.F.C. ENGINEERING COMPANY
Thermo Serv
Anoka, Minnesota 55303

NORSK
114 East 57th Street
New York, New York 10022

JOHN OSTER
    MANUFACTURING COMPANY
5055 North Lydell Avenue
Milwaukee, Wisconsin 53217

THE PIONEER RUBBER COMPANY
104 Tiffin Road
Willard, Ohio 44890

J. A. PRESTON CORPORATION
71 Fifth Avenue
New York, New York 10003

REGAL WARE, INC.
201 Second Avenue
Kewaskum, Wisconsin 53040

REHAB AIDS
5913 S. W. 8th Street
Box 612
Miami, Florida 33144

REHABILITATION EQUIPMENT, INC.
175 East 83rd Street
New York, New York 10028

REPUBLIC MOLDING CORPORATION
6330 West Touhy Avenue
Niles, Illinois 60648

RESEARCH PRODUCTS CORPORATION
1015 East Washington Avenue
Madison, Wisconsin 53702

RIVAL MANUFACTURING COMPANY
36th & Bennington
Kansas City, Missouri 64129

RONSON CORPORATION
1 Ronson Road
Woodbridge, New Jersey 07095

ROPA-MAID
Emcee Fashions
443 Kings Highway
Brooklyn, New York 11200

RUBBERMAID
1205 East Bowman
Wooster, Ohio 44692

S. A. HIRSH, *see under* HIRSH

SALTON, INCORPORATED
519 East 72nd Street
New York, New York 10021

SEARS ROEBUCK AND COMPANY
4640 Roosevelt Boulevard
Philadelphia, Pennsylvania 19132

SPARR TELEPHONE ARM COMPANY
R. D. #1, Box 241
Stroudsburg, Pennsylvania 18360

SPENCER GIFTS
Spencer Building
Atlantic City, New Jersey 08404
(General mail-order firm)

STANLEY TOOLS
480 Myrtle Street
New Britain, Connecticut 06050

STAUFFER WOOD PRODUCTS
  COMPANY
R. D. #3
Pine Grove, Pennsylvania 17963

SUBURBIA, INC.
366 Wacouta Street
St. Paul, Minnesota 55101
(General mail-order firm)

SUNBEAM CORPORATION
5400 West Roosevelt Road
Chicago, Illinois 60650

SUNSET HOUSE
Sunset Building
Beverly Hills, California 90213
(General mail-order firm)

SWING-A-WAY
  MANUFACTURING COMPANY
4100 Beck Avenue
St. Louis, Missouri 63116

THERMADOR
Division of Norris-
  Thermador Corporation
5119 District Boulevard
Los Angeles, California 90022

TOASTMASTER DIVISION
McGraw-Edison Company
1200 St. Charles Road
Elgin, Illinois 60120

VAUGHAN
  MANUFACTURING COMPANY
3311 West Carol Street
Chicago, Illinois 60600

VEL-COR, INC.
3518 West Cahuenga Boulevard
Hollywood, California 90028

VOCATIONAL GUIDANCE &
  REHABILITATION SERVICES
2239 East 55th Street
Cleveland, Ohio 44103

WALTER DRAKE AND SONS
Drake Building
Colorado Springs, Colorado 80901
(General mail-order firm)

WEAR-EVER ALUMINUM, INC.
Wear-Ever Building
Fifth at 11th Street
New Kensington,
  Pennsylvania 15068

WELMAID PRODUCTS, INC.
1529 West Armitage Avenue
Chicago, Illinois 60622

WEST BEND COMPANY
West Bend, Wisconsin 53095

WESTINGHOUSE ELECTRIC
CORP.
246 East Fourth Street
Mansfield, Ohio 44902

WESTLAND PLASTICS, INC.
Newbury Park,
California 91320

WHIRLPOOL CORP.
460 West 34th Street
New York, New York 10001

WICKLIFFE INDUSTRIES, INC.
Box 286
Wickliffe, Ohio 44092

WINCO PRODUCTS
Winfield Company, Inc.
3062 46th Avenue North
St. Petersburg, Florida 33714

WINDFALL
185 Adams Street
Bedford Hills, New York 10507

WINDOW-PAL COMPANY
6007 Euclid Avenue
Cleveland, Ohio 44123

J. WISS & SONS COMPANY
33 Littleton Avenue
Newark, New Jersey 07107

W. R. FEEMSTER, *see under*
FEEMSTER

W. R. HAUSMANN, *see under*
HAUSMANN

YIELD HOUSE
North Conway,
New Hampshire 03860
(General mail-order firm)

ZIM MANUFACTURING COMPANY
2850 West Fulton Street
Chicago, Illinois 60612

Index

From time to time new information that may be of interest or help to you will become available. In order to let you know about it and to more fully meet your needs as a homemaker, this tear-out page has been included.

We are interested in suggestions that you may want to share with others, or aids you've found helpful. Also please tell us the areas you would like to know about. If other ideas pop up later, you can always write to us at: Campbell Soup Fund, Institute of Rehabilitation Medicine, New York University Medical Center, 400 East 34th Street, New York, New York 10016, c/o Mrs. Judith Klinger, O.T.R.

NAME:
    Miss
    Mrs. _____
    Mr.

STREET OR R.F.D. _____

CITY OR TOWN _____ STATE _____ ZIP_____

AGE: _____ Under 20 _____ 20 to 35 _____ 36 to 50 _____ 51 to 65

_____ 66 to 70 _____ Over 70

HOW MANY DO YOU COOK FOR? _____ Myself _____ Husband and self

_____ Family (give number _____)

HANDICAP (if any): _____

SUGGESTIONS I HAVE FOUND HELPFUL: _____

_____

_____

_____

OTHER AREAS AND PROBLEMS I WOULD LIKE TO SEE COVERED: _____

_____